PROPERTY MANAGEMENT BASICS FOR THE PART-TIME LANDLORD

THE REAL ESTATE GUIDE FOR NEW LANDLORDS TO FINDING A GOOD TENANT, MANAGING YOUR PROPERTY, AND EVICTING THEM IF YOU HAVE TO!

G.E.S. BOLEY JR., MBA

CONTENTS

INTRODUCTION

Have you ever wondered how to get started in the rental real estate market but don't know how to? Cable television shows make "fix n' flip" seem effortless. Yet they have failed to show the nuts and bolts of the real estate management business when the cameras are off. Also, they don't go into any great detail about how to make money on your investment by holding and renting them to tenants.

Investing in the right properties at the right price and renting them out to tenants is a great way to get the most out of every dollar you spend on homes, duplexes, apartment buildings or condominium communities. It's important to understand every part of the process, whether you are investing millions of dollars or plan to start by purchasing a rental home.

Many people hold back from entering the real estate market due to a lack of good roadmaps giving direction for every part of the process from property purchase, finding the right tenant, and how to handle the situation when tenant relationships go sour. Is the thought of handling everything yourself daunting? After more than 15-years in the business, I can offer you real-life advice and useful information that's both tried and true through personal experience.

My name is George, and I am a real estate owner that successfully manages an entire portfolio of properties. I handle everything from the procurement of properties, finding the best tenants, providing the necessary maintenance, and moving forward with evictions when needed. Once you understand how the process works, you'll discover there's no need to hire an expensive property management company to oversee your rentals unless you want to. You'll have all the knowledge you need to take the real estate market by the storm.

A Growing Tenant Population

The growing need for affordable housing makes investment in the rental market an increasingly popular investment avenue. A quick snapshot of the demographics between 2006 and 2016 provided by the United States' census shows that the population grew by 23.7-million people, yet the increase in renters was 23-million. The number of homeowners only grew 700,000 during the same reporting period. More than twenty-two of the largest US cities have a larger population of renters compared to homeowners. It's a sobering set of numbers highlighting the need for rental properties of all types.

These numbers demonstrate a trend upwards in people making the decision to forego homeownership and settle in for a rental condo, apartment, or single-family home. You can enter the dynamic and energized real estate market with the understanding of your market and how the growth potential provides a better-than-average chance of getting great returns on your investment. Making the right decisions in real estate purchases and finding the best tenants are the goals of every invested person in the rental real estate market.

The Dollars and Cents of Good Real Estate Investment Decisions

How do you determine a good real estate deal from a bad one? How can you feel confident you'll make money with your rentals? I promise to answer both of these questions and more in this book. If you read this step-by-step guide and follow through with the easy-to-follow process, you too can enjoy a thriving and successful rental real estate business.

By sharing my personal experiences and words of wisdom, you'll get farther down the road of success without the same struggles many have in the business. You'll now have the essential information to refer to for guidance in nearly any circumstance arising in your tenant relationships and real estate management. Throughout the process, you have the golden opportunity to improve your credit and develop a keen sense of finding the best real estate deals your area has to offer.

Here is what a few people have to say about my level of experience and expertise:

"In my experience, George Boley has been a very upfront landlord, he is very reasonable and quick to provide a response when contacted with my concerns or problemts. George keeps his property in good running order and response to his tenants' needs appropriately always keeping communication with him open and easy."

— Jennifer M. (Tenant)

"I have known George Boley for 10 years from a local YMCA. George helped and guided me on multiple occasions with ease agreements, tenants disputes, and purchase contracts. He has been a constant resource on many of the properties I have considered with knowledge of basic inspections to property management."

— G. Borealo (Real Estate Investor)

"Mr. Boley, I am writing to tell you thank you. It's been two and a half years of wonderful living. The way you have dedicated yourself to your properties makes me feel at home. The problems I have had were resolved in such a fast manner, even late at night. I have enjoyed living in my apartment so much I have been recommending others to you.

I thank you for all the time you have put in by coming and visiting your property to make sure we don't need anything as tenets. How are you willing to always make sure our needs are met first."

— Robin G. (Former Tenant)

NOW is the Best Time to Invest in Real Estate and Learn the Secrets You Need to Succeed!

You have the prime opportunity to enter the real estate market on the ground level and propel yourself to amazing heights of success. Getting all the information you need about what to expect and how to handle all types of situations before selecting your first property is the most important step you'll take in this journey. This book is packed with everything relevant and helpful to anyone wanting to branch into real estate investments, whether it's part-time or a whole new career.

What most books fail to deliver are the actionable steps you need to take for the best results in gaining valuable property, good tenants, or how to do an actual eviction. The best landlords understand total property management is required to attract and maintain good tenants. You also have to develop a sense of when it's time to pull the plug and move towards removing a tenant. I'll give you all of the proactive steps you need to take to guarantee a better outcome in rental experiences. This will save you time and money as you manage your property.

Discover the BEST Ways to Score the Rental Properties Everyone Wants

Are you looking to pay cash for your first property? Will you need to get a mortgage? How will you make money by renting the home with a mortgage? The answer to all of these questions is in the chapters below, and I will show you how easy it is to get the numbers in balance. Learn to crunch the numbers and know when you're entering a great deal, or when to walk away.

Challenged or banged up credit is a common factor holding people back on a property deal. I can show you how to fix your credit score and improve it without paying hundreds of dollars to a credit repair company. The small amount of time and effort it takes will seem worth it when your loan approval arrives. Credit score improvement is one of the side benefits of real estate management that's helpful in every aspect of your life. It can open doors to all types of opportunities.

Rental Real Estate Ownership Allows You to Enjoy a Whole New Lifestyle

Are you looking to get more out of life than heading to the same job day after day? Making the conscious decision to become a landlord of properties is a path to freedom from the mundane. I will show you the best methods to manage your properties at a level that helps you retain good tenants, yet doesn't break the bank. You'll feel a better sense of control over your financial destiny.

The income from one well-kept rental can be life-changing for those new to the rental real estate business. Developing the skills to notice problems before they get out of hand helps protect your investment. I will teach you the signs to look for in troubled tenant situations and how to win judgments for excessive damage or vandalism. I have personally been awarded judgments in court without hiring expensive attorneys.

Are You Ready to Make Your Dreams of Rental Property Ownership and Management a Reality?

The great thing about jumping into the rental real estate business is you don't have to have tons of money or an expensive education. What you need is great management skills for time, finances, and the ability to stick within a budget. This book will lay everything out in an easy-to-understand way that allows you to start cultivating your dream right away. Some of these steps you can begin today.

What Are Your Financial Goals?

I was shocked to learn how quickly I could increase my monthly income by investing in rental real estate and managing the properties myself. I've easily made over $6,000 a month as a rookie in the field. That's over $70,000 a year I would never make without jumping into the rental real estate market.

It's smart to diversify the ways you make money and create revenue streams from many sources. How would you like to make $4,000 or $5,000 each month in rental income? How badly could your family use $10,000 extra each month? These may not be the exact amounts you set as a goal, but you WILL be equipped with the knowledge and tools you need to improve the lives of you and your family forever!

CHAPTER ONE: WHO ARE AMERICA'S LANDLORDS?

To buy or not to buy? That is probably the thought you've been battling. You've probably heard an investment expert talking about the real estate business and its financial benefits. Still, you never really knew how vast and deep it is. This chapter will provide a quick summary of the current climate in the real estate business. This is to expose you to the opportunity in the sector so that you will finally decide it is time to go all in.

Did you know that data gotten from the 2015 American Housing Survey stated that the United States has 48.5 million rental units, and 43.9 million of them are occupied? This is according to the 2015 Rental Housing Finance Survey (RHFS).

RHFS is a survey that collects data on rental properties nationwide. These data cuts across issues of finance, mortgage, management, and the physical properties of the rental properties. It is conducted every three years, and the three most recent ones are 2012, 2015, and 2018 versions. It is conducted by the Census Bureau and sponsored by the Department of Housing and Urban Development (HUD).

According to data from the Census Bureau, 36.6% of American households lived in rented homes in 2016. Over the past decade, US households have increased by 7.6 million, but the number of households owning their own houses has remained somewhat flat. This contrasts sharply with property owners that rent their property. This latter category has seen a 10% growth within the same period.

Why is this so? Some analysts have cited the increasing cost of homes and persistent fear of housing crashes as some of the foremost reasons why most Americans prefer renting to buying their homes. Others say it is because the younger generation has not accumulated enough to make down payments for their homes. Either way, the prospective landlord should see this as a win-win situation. The renters are available, and they will always be here. I hope you are getting ready to exploit this booming industry.

A survey by Trulia shows that 41% of renters listed not buying their own homes as their top regrets. I want to believe that you don't want to end up like this 41%. Instead, you should be looking to not just own your own home, but to also become a landlord so that you can tap into this massive market.

If you consider the cost of buying a home or renting it within seven years, you will be amazed that the cumulative amount is even cheaper to buy the home than renting it. David Weidner, the managing director of Tulia, confirmed this when he said, *"in every US major market, it's cheaper to buy a home than it is to rent over seven years. And it's not even close."*

If that is the case, then you, as a prospective landlord, should decide today to get buying because housing prices are on a steady increase. That means that before the seven years, the homes will appreciate even further. According to a real estate listing agency, Zillow, the median value of homes in the US was around $200,000. And that represents a whopping 7% increase from the previous year.

From all indications, renting seems to be the current trend, and that doesn't seem like it will reverse soon. Even though people consider renting is cheaper and an easily available alternative, that is no longer the case, especially in major cities, as it is becoming increasingly difficult to find suitable rentals in such cities. That says there are more renters than available homes. Does that sound like a competition? If you are conversant with the business world, then you know what competitions mean for profits.

So, who Are the Landlords?

Yes, some smart people are already rocking this industry. According to RHFS, there are two primary types of ownership of houses in the US.

The first category comprises individuals, hopefully, you and other individuals who own rental homes across the US. This group owns approximately 16.7 million properties, which contains 22.7 million units. They are often referred to as the "mom and pop" landlords. They are more likely to own smaller properties such as single-family and duplex rental homes.

The second category is the business entities. They own approximately 25.8 million units. These business entities comprise businesses, limited liability companies, partnerships, and so on. As you would expect, they own the bigger properties because they have more investment powers. They are more likely to own multifamily rental homes.

Is there a way we can determine the number of properties owned by individual investor landlords in the US? According to the RHFS 2015 report, this number is put at 16.7 million properties. That's about 75% of the total rental properties. Also, according to the Internal Revenue Service (IRS) tax data, 10.6 million taxpayers said they earned from rents in 2015 for 17.7 million properties.

Seeing that the number of properties is quite close, we can conclude that the number of properties owned by individual investors is around 17 to 18 million, owned by around 10 million to 11 million individual investor landlords. These 10 to 11 million people cannot be wrong. There must be some massive benefits to it, and I hope you will soon join the smart investors.

If we compared the 75% individual investor ownership of properties for 2015 to 91.6% in 1991, we would see that business entities have seen the numerous real estate benefits. Hence they are increasing their stake in it. I am sure you know that no business entity is willing to feature in a venture that is not profitable. If they are doing it, with all their expertise in business, you and I should be doing it.

Other Interesting Statistics in the World of Real Estate

• Out of the 100 largest cities in the US, 91 of them have witnessed a rent increase over the last year. This statistic is according to ApartmentList, which they published in their national rent index. This is not surprising because landed properties are always appreciating with time. For instance, Sacramento in California experienced the highest growth in rent with a whopping 9.3% increase.

• 32% of renters are renting because it is a thing of choice for them, whereas 65% does so for financial reasons. From this statistic, you can see that it is not all renters that can't afford to buy their homes. Some Americans just prefer to be tenants than owning their properties. So, yes, there is no running short of renters. Even if every American suddenly has enough money to buy their homes, some will still choose to stay in rental homes. There is no ending for real estate. There will always be people who own homes in one state or city and might require to stay temporarily in another city or state. There will also be businesses looking for rental units so they can run their businesses from there.

• Renters spend more of their income on rents. According to data published by SmartMove, there are indications that rents are stretching renters. The median US rent accounts for about 29.1% of what a typical household earns. It used to be 25.8% in 2000, according to Zillow.

How Much Can an Average Landlord Make Off One House?

If you know a little about real estate and all its variables, then you know there is no straight answer. Lots of factors such as property type, crime rate, job opportunities, and presence of amenities, among other things, influence the rent rates across different locations in the country. Simply put, I cannot tell you "an average landlord makes "$X" in a month, no one can, and that's because it varies with the variables mentioned here. We will look at these variables in the next chapter and see how they affect rental rates.

Now, even though we can't have a fixed rate, I will try to provide you with an average guide of your expected income as a landlord so that you will have an idea of what you are expecting.

According to ZipRecruiter, the landlord's national average salary is pegged at $73,695. This is as of June 1, 2020. This is only an average of the extremes. For instance, some landlords earn as high as $121,000, and some earn as low as $27,500. ZipRecruiter reports that the majority of landlords in the US earn between $46,500 and $100,000, which represents the 25th percentile and 75th percentile, respectively.

Why Should You Own a Rental Property?

Now you have seen some real-time data on the real estate industry, and I do hope you see the impressive prospects. Now let's get more practical and see some other clear-cut reasons why you should be looking in the direction of real estate.

Generally speaking, you know how it is more pennywise to own assets that can generate income than piling up assets that generate expenses. Well, there is no better example of income-generating assets than investment in real estate.

You know that if you buy a house to live in, you will incur some expenditures by way of maintenance, taxes, repairs, mortgage interest, and some other associated expenses such as homeowner association fees or even land-scaping. But when that property is for rent, as in real estate, you will still settle some of these expenses and still end up with positive cash flow because you will be generating income from it.

I believe you have heard that saying, "time is money," I can confidently tell you that saying is truer when you are a landlord. Being a landlord brings lots of responsibilities and financial obligations, but when you look at the time value of properties, the requirements become almost insignificant.

Benefits of Real Estate

From everything we've been discussing, you know that real estate can grant you financial freedom because it can guarantee a steady income. The best part is you can be on your 9-5 job and try your hands on real estate. Then whenever you feel like your income from it can sustain you, you can decide to quit your job to become a full-time real estate investor.

Here are some of the benefits of investing in real estate:

- **Steady Income**

The real estate industry is one that is so reliable. If you do your research before sealing the deals, the properties you purchase will generate income for you steadily. If one property can cover your costs and still leave some money on the table for you, now imagine if you invest in multiple real estate projects. You might soon be achieving the financial life of your dreams sooner than you expect.

- **Long Term Financial Security**

We've seen parents who die and will estates to their children and grandchildren. Some of those properties were purchased a long time ago, and they've reaped from it all the days of their life. Now their offspring will continue from where they stopped. Such is the power of real estate.

It becomes even more appealing when we factor in the appreciation that these properties will undergo for the period they will be yours. With an investment in real estate, an investor can derive a sense of financial security because there is a constant inflow of money, and it is not stopping anytime soon.

- **Tax Benefits**

A tax benefit is the government's way of telling you that they love what you are doing. As an investor in real estate, the government grants you some tax exemptions. That is why your rental income will not be subjected to self-employment taxation. Additionally, you will also get tax breaks from the government for property depreciation, maintenance, repairs, insurance, etc. To top it all, you also get a lower tax rate for your long term investments.

• Covers For Your Mortgage

As the tenants pay their rents, you can use some from it to pay your mortgage gradually, while keeping some for yourself. So we can conclude that real estate makes it possible for you to get a person or people that will gradually pay off your mortgage until the property becomes debt-free.

• Inflation

Real estate can serve as a hedge against inflation. It can shield you from the troubling effects of inflation because as inflation bites hard, your rental income increases to accommodate for those effects. The value of your property also appreciates with inflation. When you become a real estate investor, you will join this special group of people that welcomes inflation with open arms because they know it's more valuable for their properties.

• Independence

Most people are trapped in 9-5 jobs that bore them to death. Some others hardly have time to do the things they love because their jobs take up their time. Even though it requires some effort from you, real estate can still be seen as a passive income. You can combine it with fun and family time as you can finally be able to do the things you love.

There is also the added advantage of autonomy, control,

and exclusive right to it. With it, you are the absolute shots callers and the ultimate decision-maker. As you start off, you get to decide the properties to invest in and the ones to skip. You also decide on the tenants to accommodate and the ones that you won't.

- **Real Estate Leverage**

The real estate industry makes it possible for you to use several financial instruments to your advantage. For instance, you can access borrowed capital or mortgage to increase your investment power. Banks and other loaning agencies will be willing to give you a loan because your other properties will serve as collateral. The important thing is getting your first property. From there, everything becomes lots easier.

Inherent Risks in Real Estate

I started by explaining how massive the real estate market is by showing you verified statistics on the industry, and now I just showed you some benefits too. Still, since I promised to bare it all, I won't fail to inform you of the inherent risks in the business. I hear you exclaiming, "Risks?" Well, yes! Risks. Every business has got its fair share of risks, and real estate is not an exception. But the good news is these risks can be mitigated to the barest minimum.

So, why is real estate risky?

Here is why.

Just like stocks, buildings too can lose value. I know we talked about how properties appreciate generally, but they can lose value too. Not to talk of natural disasters that could claim properties when they occur.

There is also the risk of a prolonged vacancy, a landlord's nightmare. That you have a property doesn't mean that you will have customers competing to stay in them. They will be those times when some apartments will be empty, but to mitigate this risk, ensure that you buy strategic properties after considering the factors we will discuss in chapter two of this book.

There is also the risk of undertaking costly repairs and maintenance that you never anticipated. That may impact your cash flow negatively.

You can also encounter a troublesome tenant that may even sue you. But you can mitigate this risk by paying up your insurance and also getting your legal protection. Or better still, take proactive steps to prevent that from happening by carefully screening your prospective tenants before accommodating them.

I hope that our discussion so far has opened your eyes to the numerous real estate opportunities. The statistics don't lie, and the current trends will continue and even get better for the property earners. So what other excuse do you have now? This book will give you all the knowledge you need to do this effectively, so I want to believe that you will be acquiring your first property after reading this book.

CHAPTER TWO: GETTING STARTED AND LOOKING AT BUYING YOUR FIRST HOME

In case you are still skeptical about this whole real estate thing, here is a little statistic to help you decide. According to a market analysis by Zillow, landlords received a cumulative of $478.5 billion from renters in 2016. In 2019, three years later, that amount had risen to $512 billion, representing an increase of $33.5 billion in just three years. Going by this rate, imagine what the amount will be in some five years from today.

Now that you have seen the immense opportunities available to you in the real estate business let me walk you through everything you need to start and kill this thing. First of all, I want you to discard every view you've had about real estate before now. Maybe you've told yourself that it is too complicated and difficult, and you may not be built for it. Let me inform you that most of the numbers of private individuals who own and run rental homes are regular people like you and me.

While you may require education to excel in this business, it must not be a college degree in real estate management. A book like this one that will give you a tour of the industry will suffice. From when you start, you can begin to improve your "*landlording*" skills with firsthand experience.

But first, let's get you started.

Before you venture into this business, there are a couple of things you must consider. While this book may ease your journey through the world of real estate, do not expect a rosy ride. It comes with lots of pressure of its own, but it is nothing you can't handle. So here are some tips and questions that can make your transition easier.

1. The Necessary Investment to Start

As you probably already know, the real estate business is a capital-intensive one. So you must answer the key question, "Do I have the necessary investment power to buy a property?" It is not like there are no other options, but the business is better when you have the money to buy your property exclusively. For instance, you may opt to seek mortgage for your property, but that would mean battling mortgage payments when you finally start. And mind you, apart from these mortgage repayments, there is also the issue of maintenance and occasional repairs. If mortgage repayment is not giving room for profits after some other expenses, a real estate business may fail.

It is not like you must have the entire money to buy a property outrightly, but it guarantees you a positive cash flow if you can do that.

2. Rent Vs. Expenses

The goal of any business is to be profitable in the long run, and real estate is not an exception. You must ensure that your real estate business can generate enough income for you to be profitable. You will have to answer the key question,

"Will I be able to charge enough rent that can cover my expenses?" You must consider some variables such as location, competition, and the prevailing pricing flexibility. For instance, if your goal is to earn a living from your rental property, you should ensure that your monthly income guarantees you at least $50,000 annually to earn you a living. But if you are going to be struggling with stiff competition and still have mortgage fees to pay off, you may end up with a profit that is short of that.

So, you must weigh your options and verify that your investment will be profitable, although, more often than not, that is usually the case, it is good you do your homework and verify. Later in this book, I will show you how to go about this.

3. Relating With People

Becoming a landlord means that you will relate to tenants, contractors, other landlords, and the rest. If you know how to handle people, you stand a better chance of winning in this game. In your real estate career, you will encounter some difficult tenants, and since they have legal rights, you must proceed with caution when dealing with them. We will still take a more in-depth look at the issue of tenant handling later in this book, but for now, just know that if you must excel in this business, you need to know how to relate with people.

Features That Make For A Profitable Rental Property

As you set off to acquire your first property, there are some features you must consider. You should realize that buying a property is a major decision for you regardless of whether this is the first time you are buying or your fifth time. Since it is a major decision, it should be treated accordingly. That means you must weigh your options and decisions regarding issues of location, mortgage, payments, and others. properly. That way, you will ensure that you do not get yourself and your investment money tied up in a property for more than 12 to 15 years.

Now let's look at some of these features you should consider carefully before deciding. They include:

• Neighborhood

The neighborhood you choose for your property determines two key things: the types of tenant you will attract and the vacancy rate you will record with your property. For instance, if you buy a property close to a school, then chances are that most of your tenants will be students. But if it is in an industrial area, chances are they may be factory workers. While the property in the industrial area will have a decent inflow of tenants year in and year out, that will not be the case with the property in a school neighborhood because summer may affect tenant availability.

• Property Taxes

Property taxes are those taxes you will pay for your property. They vary from area to area. Before making your purchase, ensure that the property taxes of your target area is friendly. Also, find out the exact sum and see if it is an amount you can pay comfortably and still manage to have a positive cash flow.

Note that property taxes can be high for some great neighborhoods that can attract and keep long-term tenants that will pay good rents to you. In such a case, you can cope with the property tax since you will still be profitable in the long run. In contrast, some unappealing neighborhoods will still charge massively by way of property taxes. You don't want to buy your properties in such areas as it can drastically reduce your profits.

To access the tax information for the various neighborhoods, you can check the municipality's assessment office. Alternatively, you can talk to other homeowners in your target neighborhood.

While conducting your findings, keep an eye out for potential increases in the future. See if there are indications or talks of a possible hike in the nearest future. For instance, if a neighborhood or town is in the middle of financial distress, they may look to property taxes to cushion the effects of such distress.

- **Schools**

The presence of quality schools in a neighborhood makes it appealing for families. Schools here don't refer to just colleges or universities, high schools, preschools and other forms of schooling are also inclusive. Families would prefer neighborhoods where their children and dependents can have quality education. Keep this in mind when choosing your prospective location.

Even if you decide that you want to sell off your property someday, the presence of quality schools around will make it more appealing to buyers.

- **Crime Rate**

We know that some people will manage to stay in neighborhoods ridden with crime, mostly due to their financial status. Families that have alternatives will never settle for neighborhoods with a high crime rate. As you scout for prospective properties, check and compare the crime rates because nobody loves to be at the center of crime.

The local police station, realty websites, or library will keep data on crime rates. Common things to look out for are vandalism, theft, burglary, and other petty and serious crimes. You might also want to talk to other homeowners in the location. Ask them about how frequently the police visit the neighborhood. You should also see if the crime rates within some period have been increasing or decreasing. If it is on the rise, then it can get worse in the nearest future. But if it is declining, then the neighborhood will be desirable in the nearest future.

- **Job Availability**

Naturally, people are drawn to areas with job opportunities. This is the cause of overpopulation in major cities. Luckily for you, you can check the job availability of an area when you visit the US Bureau of Labor Statistics either online or in their offices. This information can also be found at the local library servicing such an area. You can also conduct a google search of businesses in the neighborhood. Or if you hear that any big business is moving to that place, you can look to invest there because such a move will attract people. Such announcements can also cause housing prices to increase.

- **Availability of Social Amenities**

You want to be sure that your prospective location has basic amenities such as movie theaters, stadiums, gyms, restaurants, amusement parks, and other perks that can make the place a great place to inhabit. You can tour the neighborhood to find out for yourself or ask people who are already residing there. You can also visit city halls or local tour guides to get an idea of the available amenities and where they are concentrated so that you can buy strategically.

- **Development Potentials**

If there are strong indications or plans for development in an area, look to buy a property there. You can get such information from the municipal planning department. They will provide you with the details of the developments that have been zoned to such an area. Also, if you notice that lots of construction projects are ongoing in such areas, it could be investors preparing themselves for the upcoming development. Apart from that, the constructions will also lead to more developments making the properties in the area to appreciate in value.

- **Listings and Vacancy Rates**

If you do your homework properly, you can save yourself from bad real estate investments. For instance, if you can research the fates of people who own properties in the area already, you will not make the same mistakes they made. One way to do this is to look at the vacancy rates of such an area. If you notice a remarkably high number of listings, it could indicate that the neighborhood is declining and people are leaving, causing the landlords to list more openings and declare more vacancies.

Generally, you want vacancy rates to be low because that is only when you and other landlords can raise rental rates.

- **The Average Rent for Such Area**

The rent is the best part of this whole thing. It is your

reward for all the research and investment. As a result, you must ensure that it is worth it. Like I said earlier, your rent should be enough to take care of other expenses such as taxes, repairs, renovations, and still have enough for you to live on. Otherwise, it is not worth it. That is why you must pay close attention to the average rent. Ensure that you know the prevailing rates, taxes, and what the future holds by looking at the prevailing trends for sometimes now.

- **Natural Disasters**

Some areas are more prone to natural disasters than others. You need to avoid such areas as much as you can. Check if the area suffers from any of the natural disasters such as earthquakes, floods, volcanoes, and tsunamis. If that is the case, you just might lose your property to these natural disasters should they occur. I like to avoid areas with cases of natural disasters.

Again, you can lose a part of your rental income to cover costs if you purchase a property in a disaster-prone area. You might also record some vacancies because people will normally avoid those areas because they fear their safeties and the safety of their properties.

Information on all the factors we have discussed can be gotten from appropriate bodies scattered all over the country. Still, it is always a good idea to talk to residents directly. They may have more recent and accurate information for you. After all, they are experiencing these things first hand.

What Type of Property Should You Start With?

Although this is largely dependent on your investment power. Generally, if this is your first time venturing into real estate, consider condominiums or single-family apartments.

The reason is that they are the most rented types of properties. Condos have the added advantage of presenting you with lesser maintenance cost as the condo association will usually take care of the external repairs, while you worry about the interior.

On the other hand, single-family homes will attract long-term renters for you. Single-family homes have the added advantage of getting your families or couples as tenants. This category of renters is generally less problematic since they are more financially stable and law-abiding. That way, you can be sure of timely rent payments.

After you have narrowed down on the neighborhood and the type of property to invest in, the next thing to focus on should be the appreciation factor for such a property.

But, how do you know a property that has appreciation prospects? Look for strategic properties that are lacking from a few cosmetic changes. It could be that the paintings or fittings are outdated. When you purchase such property and rehab it, you will attract fresh tenants, and you can afford to increase the rent. Just make sure that the rental property satisfies the other factors we have considered. Housing flipping will grant you the golden opportunity to sell your property at a higher rate should you ever decide to sell-off.

Another key thing to consider is the amount you are paying to acquire the property. If you get this wrong, you can as well kiss your chances of profitability goodbye. Ensure that whichever property you are settling for is a reasonably priced one. As a general guide, do not pay more money than you hope to get from 12 times the annual rent. If you cannot recover the amount you invested in a 12-year window, then I doubt that it is a profitable venture.

To better your chances of buying at the right price, work with professional property value tools like an appraisal or like rehabilitated property comparisons called COMPS in the industry, especially now that you are starting. Valuing a property on your own can be tricky because the seller will be looking to get as much money they can for their property, but you must never allow that to happen. There are other properties in the same neighborhood that can offer you a better deal.

By all means, ensure you end up with an asset and not a liability. If you critically look at it, you will agree with me that we have two types of houses in the real estate business, and they are assets or liabilities. Let me explain. An example of an asset is a house that helps you with the payment like a duplex, triplex, or quad-plex in which you live in one unit, and your tenant or tenants live in the other or others, paying your rent and contributing to your mortgage payment. An asset takes 100% of the monthly burden from you and spreads it out amongst your tenant or tenants.

In contrast, an example of a liability is a house that you buy with or without your spouse's financial help, and YOU are solely responsible for the monthly mortgage. That takes money from you instead of making it available for you.

Conclusively, the outcome of your real estate business is largely dependent on your diligent research. You want to be sure that any property you are settling for is in the right state, city, and neighborhood. The final piece to the puzzle is ensuring that you end up with the right property. You don't want to disadvantage yourself from the onset. Your aim of going into real estate is to be profitable, and if thorough research can grant you that, then don't sleep on it.

CHAPTER THREE: HOW TO DO YOUR CREDIT REPAIR

If you are super rich and can buy your first rental property without a mortgage or any other form of a loan, that will be great. But if you do not have all the money you need to buy a rental property all by yourself, something can still be done. You can fall back to the good old mortgage, make a down payment of 20%, and pay the rest 80% by installment. You can also seek other forms of loans to acquire more properties as you begin to expand in your new business. But your chances of landing a good rate largely depends on your credit score.

In this chapter, I will explain what credit score is, and show you how you can repair it so that you can get the best mortgage rate offers around. I will also show you the importance of a good credit score, generally. For instance, do you know that a credit score of 300 to 579 may not make the number work for you when you want to buy a rental property?

Come with me. Let's explore the credit score and how to get the best out of it.

But, first, what is the credit score?

A credit score is a number that shows a consumer's creditworthiness. It ranges from 300 to 850. If your credit score is high, it tells creditors that you are trustworthy, and you are more likely to repay your debt in due time. Hence, they will be willing to take fewer interest rates when they borrow money. In contrast, if your credit score is low, they will charge you more interest rates to compensate for the greater risk they are taking by lending you money.

Your credit score is arrived at by looking at your credit history. Your credit history includes the number of accounts you have, your total debts, length of credit history, types of loan, and your repayment history.

This method of estimating an individual's creditworthiness was developed by Fair Isaac Corporation (FICO), and most financial institutions in the country are now using it. The one developed by FICO is not the only one out there, but it is the most widely used one.

Three agencies in the US report credit records and they are Experian, Equifax, and Transunion. These agencies are responsible for storing, updating, and reporting consumer's credit histories.

It is graded as follows:

- 800 to 850: Excellent
- 740 to 799: Very Good
- 670 to 739: Good
- 580 to 669: Fair
- 300 to 579: Poor

Generally, creditors consider people with credit scores below 640 as subprime borrowers. Accessing funds on credit is difficult for these people, and when they do, it comes at a higher than usual rate. Sometimes, they may give them a short term to repay their loan, and they may even require them to provide a co-signer just to access credit.

You don't want to be in that position as an intending real estate investor. You need all the credit points you can get so that funds can be easily available to you. You want to be targeting a credit score of 700 and above as this will afford you lower interest rates, more funds, and a longer repayment schedule.

A credit score is also important for other things other than for obtaining funds; it can also be used to determine the initial amount an individual can pay for a gadget such as a smartphone, computer, or even house rent. So, yes, it is very important.

Now, how can we make yours better?

The thing with credit scores is that most people never really try to make it better until they need it. However, the irony is that the credit score cannot be changed overnight, so the best time to start is now. If you do not fix it soon, when it is time for you to buy your house, you may need to save yourself a lot of money due to bad or average credit. So you must fix your credit before you start looking for a loan or getting pre-qualified.

There are two broad ways of doing this; the first is to pay a credit repair company to fix it up for you while you pay them a fee. The second option is to do it yourself. We will look at both of them briefly so you can choose whichever method suits you.

There are several credit repair companies you can pay to help you repair your credit score, but I think you should do it yourself because it is very easy, and that is what credit repair companies don't want you to know. Besides, don't fall for the lie that it can be repaired overnight, it actually takes time.

If you still wish to go with credit repair companies, they

are obligated to only receive payment from you after delivering results. However, you might be required to pay an initial setup fee and follow up with monthly fees as the company delivers on the goods. Expect to pay between the $10 to $100 for the setup fee and between $30 to $100 for monthly payments.

How to Repair Your Credit Yourself

Let's look at how it is calculated before we start looking at how you can improve your scores. This will give you a better understanding of the whole thing.

An individual's credit score is dependent on the five factors below:

1. Payment history: The payment history is an indication of the time it takes a consumer to pay his\her debt. Longer payment history is undesirable because it says that the individual might do the same or worse with the one at hand. It accounts for 35% of a credit score.

2. The total amount owed: The total amount owed focuses on credit utilization, which is the percentage of credit available to a consumer that is currently being used. For instance, a person might be entitled to $1,000, and they are currently using $500. That puts their credit utilization at 50% because they are using half of what they can normally use. The more of your credit you are using, the lesser your credit score because it says you are deep into debt. The total amount owed accounts for 30% of the credit score.

3. Length of credit history: A longer length of credit history gives your creditor some confidence, and they

consider lending you money as less risky. It also tells them that there is more data to determine your payment history accurately. It accounts for 15% of one's credit score.

4. Types of credit: This indicates whether or not an individual has a mix of installment credits. Possible installment credits are mortgage and car loans venture. Revolving credits such as credit cards are also included. Usually, the more the mix, the lower your credit score because, again, it shows you have got a complex web of debts to sort. It accounts for 10% of the entire credit score.

5. New credit: It factors in the number of new accounts an individual has, it also shows the time that the more recent account was opened. This accounts for the remaining 10% of the consumer's credit score.

Now that you know how it is estimated, let's look at some ways you can use to repair your credit score without recruiting the services of a credit repair company.

Know Your Score

You can get your credit report when you create an account with Credit Karma (Has Both Transunion and Equifax), and Experian. It is 100% free to sign up with them. Once you set up your account, you can request your credit report since they are required to provide you a free copy. With each of the reports, there might be slight differences, but generally, the entries should be the same irrespective of the custodian you are getting it from.

Dispute Negative Marks

When you get your score report, you might notice something off. It could be a mistake of some sort. Such a mark will negatively affect your score, so you must report it with the hopes of removing it.

How do you remove that incident from your report? Well, first, it has to be true and an honest fact. What does that mean? It is possible that you might have had a charge in your account, which you paid off accordingly, but now, you just found out that it is still there. Yes, it is your charge on your report, but you paid it off. If the incident does not show "paid off," you can request that it be updated or removed from your credit report, and they have to do it. It is possible that the fault is not yours as mix-ups can occur, especially with people with the same name.

Formerly, before they made it digital, consumers had to write letters to the credit bureau informing them of errors in their credit records that they wanted to dispute. But now, disputing errors is lots easier as you can do it on the website of the credit bureaus or even on other free services such as Credit Karma.

When sorting your dispute, focus on those ones that weigh more. You have seen how different items of the credit report affect your credit score, so you should know the factors that weigh more heavily.

To ensure you spot any error no matter how small, check personal information such as name, address, social security number, and then your credit history. When checking your credit history, review all your credit cards, check outstanding debts, and your major purchases.

If, in the process of checking, you spot a mistake, make a copy of your report and highlight every error you have noticed. Then get a copy of any document you can use to back your claim of error. This is what the credit bureaus will look at to verify the authenticity of your claims.

Attach the copies to a letter which you will address to the specific credit reporting agency that made a mistake. In the letter, explain the mistake as clearly as possible and refer them to the backing documents that you have attached. They should get back to you with their resolution within 30 days.

Once you file for a dispute, and it is yet to be removed, it has to be updated to say something like "under review" or "under dispute." This is a tip many people with bad credit use to get the incidents off their credit reports or in transit while their report is being pulled for other purchases or investments. So you simply write two letters, one to the company that filed this incident with the credit company requesting an "investigation" use the word "INVESTIGA-TION" into the payment history of this account because it has been settled but has not been updated on your credit report. Then you write a second letter to the credit reporting company or companies telling them you filed a complaint about an investigation into this. Attach a copy of your letter to the business as proof and attach your evidence, either a bill or receipt voided check, money order, or whatever you used to pay and settle this account.

Personally, I use Credit Karma to get an idea of what's on my personal credit report and what I have to get off. They also give me an outlook as to my score from all two credit bureaus. That way, I can stay current and pick out any abnormality to my scores so I can do something about it.

1. Cut Down on Things that Hurt Your Score

With your score known, possible disputes removed, it is time to stop the bleeding. How do you stop the bleeding? Quit spending beyond your budget. Start thinking like an investor because that is what you are now. Again, always have your credit score in mind when transacting because you need it to access the best credits in your business.

Ensure that you pay your bills on time, if you have pending debts, do well to pay them off, do not apply for unnecessary credits, at least not now, apply when you are ready to start investing.

I know it is not going to come easy, especially if you are not earning more than enough, but if you can learn the habit of budgeting, you will improve your scores. Budgeting is quite simple. Just review monthly returns and your monthly expenses. Subtract your expenses from your income and see how you are doing. If you are running on negative, then you are running on debts. Cut down on expenses and ensure that your expenses are within your income, and you still have some savings after all your expenses.

2. Increase Your Credit Limit

Card utilization is another factor that can impact your credit score substantially. It is the ratio of the credit available to you, to the credit you are currently utilizing. It is always good to keep this ratio above 50%. For instance, if your available limit is $6,000 in your credit account, keep your debt below $3,000 to achieve that 50%. Never max out your cards because it will affect your score.

You can also use a more proactive approach to increasing your credit limit. For the example above, if you increase your limit to $9,000 while using $3,000, your card utilization improves to around 67%, which is very good for your credit score.

If you've been keeping a good payment history, you can get your credit card company to increase your limit. They will be willing to do that because they even want you to carry a high balance.

You can also improve your card utilization percentage by opening another credit card account. When you open it, and you are disciplined enough not to carry a balance on it, the available credit in this new card increases your limit and improves your credit score. When choosing a new card to open, go for one that doesn't charge an annual fee, so you don't accrue unnecessary debts. You can get such an account by opening it in a bank where you already have an account. Some might argue that cards without annual fees charge higher, but since you won't be taking out any credits, the charges have nothing on you.

In the same vein, keep your "old" cards, don't close them. Closing them decreases your overall average credit history, and you have seen how credit history impacts your card. Keep your old cards in a safe place, and check from time to time.

After increasing your balance, be wise. Realize that your goal of increasing this limit is to better your score, not to rope yourself in more debt and further hurt your score. Don't spend on frivolities, know the difference between your needs and your wants, and stick to your budget always. If you know you just can't do this even if you try, then this point is not an option for you.

3. Try A Less Conventional Method

You can also try something else that credit repair companies do. Although it is not the best approach. However, let me share so you have a comprehensive knowledge of everything you can try. You know how you can disprove inaccurate information on your credit record. This method involves disproving accurate ones, too, with hopes that the creditor will not reply to the request that the credit bureaus will send to them to verify the authenticity of your claim. Usually, when you make such claims, the credit bureau will ask the creditor to verify. In some cases, they will, but several collection agencies won't reply. If they don't, the bureau will have no other option but to remove that entry from your credit report.

How Credit Score Affect You as a Real Estate Investor

By now, you know credit score can decide the rates you get for credits but is that all it means for you as a real estate investor? No, that's not all. Bringing it home to you and intending real estate investors, let's look at how your credit score can impact your mortgage rates.

- ### Loan-To-Value Ratio (LTV)

LTV is an important factor in the real estate business. It is the percentage of the cost price of a property that you can get credit for. For instance, if your LTV is 90%, then you can get a loan of $90,000 for a sale price of $100,000. Do you see how important this is? With a good LTV, you can purchase properties with other people's money, and it all boils down to your credit score.

- ### Access to Programs

As a real estate investor, you want to be able to access every possible credit program in your niche. A bad credit score can deny you this luxury, and you mustn't allow that to happen.

- ### Bad Credit Score Can Affect Private Mortgage Insurance (PMI)

The rate you will pay for your PMI can be influenced by your credit score. The PMI is very important because lenders will require you to carry a PMI if your down payment for a loan is going to be less than 20%.

For the calculation of your PMI, insurance companies also consider your credit score. For instance, if your credit score is 760 or more, you will be charged at a rate of 5.4% for a 95% loan that has a 30% coverage.

Summarily, a good credit score is very desirable for any intending real estate investor because it makes it easier for them to access funds. It is possible that you don't know what your score is now, but that is where to start. Start now and fix it, because the earlier, the better. If you are waiting for when you are ready to invest in real estate, you will be disappointed when you discover that it is not something you can fix overnight.

CHAPTER FOUR: BUYING YOUR INVESTMENT PROPERTY

To "Incorporate" or not to "Incorporate?" That is the Question

Disclaimer: I AM NOT AN ACCOUNTANT OR A LAWYER. ANY INFORMATION IN THE BOOK SHOULD BE TAKEN AND USED FOR INFORMATION PURPOSES ONLY!!! YOU SHOULD ALWAYS CONSULT A LAWYER AND OR ACCOUNTANT WHEN CONSIDERING ANY BUSINESS DECISION.

You've gotten pre-qualified for your first home, and you know the difference between an asset and liability. So, I am sure you are ready to buy an asset now. But now, there is a little detail you have to worry about. If you haven't thought about it and your accountant or lawyer hasn't mentioned it to you, you should think about if you want to own this asset as a sole owner. Meaning you own it by yourself and all the liability is yours. Any corporate business protection laws do not protect you. Or you want to incorporate and buy the house as an income-producing asset for your company. There are three forms of companies to pick from, such as S. Corps, C-Corp, Limited Liability Companies.

What Does it Mean to Incorporate?

There are three broad categories through which a business can be owned. They are sole proprietorship, partnership, and corporation. In a sole proprietorship, there is hardly a separation between your name and that of your business as you own the business personally, and you have the exclusive right to decide what goes on in the business. But you are also liable for the debts and losses that your business might incur.

A partnership is more or less a sole proprietorship, but this time, it is not just one person. Here the liability of the business is jointly owned by the partners of the business.

However, our interest here is the third category, which is a corporation. When you incorporate, you make your real estate business a legal entity capable of buying, owning, and leasing properties. It is also capable of getting sued or suing others in the course of business. It can enter and dissolve contracts. Once it gets chartered by the state where you are operating, your real estate business will have its rights, assets, liabilities that are separate from the ones you have.

When it comes to deciding whether to incorporate it, there is no one size fits all to it. That which is suitable for you might not be suitable for me. So it is always better to speak to your lawyer and accountant about it. They will help you decide on the one that suits you best. If you don't have either, speak to your bookkeeper about it to weigh the pros and cons of incorporating or not.

However, I will be sharing some of the advantages and disadvantages of incorporation to prepare you for that talk with your lawyer or accountant.

Benefits of Incorporation

Here are some of the benefits you stand to gain if you incorporate your real estate business:

Personal Liability

Incorporation enables you to separate yourself from your business. By incorporating, you are making your business a legal entity that is recognizable by law. If your business gets sued for any reason, it will face its lawsuit. And if the business gets into debt, it will face it on its own. Without incorporation, you will be financially liable for these possible issues. Meaning that your assets can be taken away if the business runs into trouble.

Generally, your involvement in the real estate sector means you will be handling a substantial amount of accounts, so you understand the magnitude of debts and lawsuits in this sector. You may be liable for damages and debts of thousands of dollars, so, yes, you need protection which incorporation can grant you.

Before you can enjoy this liberty, you must have transferred your property to the corporation you've formed. Without that, you remain the property's legal owner. Hence, you will answer for any lawsuits. Then after incorporating, you must abide by the corporate law regulations.

According to experts, some instances can still make your asset vulnerable in the case of debt or payment of damages. Let's use the next few lines to look at those instances.

• If you signed it. Sometimes, when you go to lending agencies as a corporation, they may require you to sign that you will pay back the loan if your business can't. If you accept such terms, then your assets may still be vulnerable.

• If the legal action is directed against you.

• If in the process of running your business, you step on an unforgiving toe in a manner that can be deemed to be outside the jurisdiction of the business, and they sue you, not the business, then you will be liable for it.

• Also, in a case where the business is criminally negligent, the corporation's key personnel can be held personally liable.

• A concept, known as piercing the corporate veil which stipulates that your asset, as the owner, can be threatened if it is discovered that you have not properly set up your business. The argument, thereof, is that you and your business are the same. Hence, your assets can be used to settle a judgment.

To prevent piercing the corporate veil or other occurrences that can threaten your personal assets, the *Small Business Advisor* magazine advises that you do the following things:

• Keep up with your taxes.

• Keep to regulatory requirements always.

• Comply with corporate minutes and all the organizational bylaws (have your lawyer tell you all that is applicable in your location).

• Let your personal account be separate from your business account and keep it like that at all times.

• Keep a healthy debt-to-equity ratio as this puts you in a good spot in terms of capitalization.

It Makes Accessing of Funds Easier

Once you incorporate your real estate business, it tells lending institutions that you are very serious about your business enterprise because it simply says you are ready to devote more time and resources to your business. That, coupled with the fact that you will be required to report financial performance from time to time, will make them consider you more favorably. Again, lending institutions will know that you can access more funds, even if not from them. Hence, your chances of remaining solvent are higher. As a result, they will prefer to lend you money.

Apart from borrowing from lending institutions, another source of capital that is available to corporations is the selling of company shares to investors, making them part owners of the business. If this is a road you will like to walk, then the corporation is perfect for you.

Easier Process of Ownership Transfer

This is done by selling company stock to the intending new owner. If you consider this as an advantage, then a corporation might just be suitable for you.

It Makes Business Deductions Possible

As a corporation, you can subtract up to 100% of operating costs such as insurance and salaries from company profits before allocating your profits and that of other owners.

It Grants Privacy

If you incorporate your business, you can keep your identity secret if that is what you want. This is especially important for tenants because it makes it easier to work with them. They will not take you for granted, as they will assume that you are an employee of the company that manages their home. This will prevent them from wanting to bargain or making late payments, especially for people that might have a personal relationship with you.

Tax Expenses

Tax cuts? Yes, that, too, is one of the perks of incorporating because it allows you to save on your taxes. Normally, as a private owner, you cannot subtract home office space expenses and other related expenses from your personal tax return, but as a corporation, you can do that. You can still save more on tax by electing subchapter S tax status so you won't be taxed for corporate profits and dividends.

Legitimacy and Professionalism

You tend to do better with tenants when they believe that they are dealing with a legitimate business entity. That can make you attract high-quality tenants to your business, since, by incorporating, your business appears more reputable.

Disadvantages

Cost of Lawsuits

While some people believe that a business that is a legal entity is good for protecting you from lawsuits, you can still be liable in some rare cases. Besides, if you purchase your properties as a sole owner, you can represent yourself in court proceedings. If you incorporate, you have to hire a lawyer to represent you. This can be very expensive for removal or eviction.

Cost and Complexity of Administration

If it is just you running your thing, you would normally just do your thing alone and pay yourself, but as you incorporate, you will need a bookkeeper, an accountant, and possibly a lawyer to handle all required accounting records so your company can produce your annual financial statements. And to think that corporations are governed by several regulations at local, state, and even federal levels, you know that's one hell of a lot of paperwork.

There are also the legal costs of incorporating which you will incur by the several filings you will have to make as required by the Business Incorporation Act. Then there is the fee that comes with incorporation, which you wouldn't have incurred if you operated on your own or as a partnership.

Double Taxation

If you register your real estate business as a C corporation, you may be subjected to double taxation. It is double because you, your company, will pay taxes on its profits, then you will still pay tax again on the declared dividends accruing from your stock in the business. That is because it is considered that you are receiving financial compensations in two ways, which is true. The two ways are, first, your payment for your services to the business, then your share of the declared dividends. However, if you make it an S-corporation, you might be able to escape this double taxation.

Separation of Finance

While separation of your finances from that of the business is vital for protecting your assets from issues the business might face, it can also be considered a disadvantage. And that's because you cannot just wake up one morning, see a car you love and dip hands in the corporation's purse to purchase it. Although, judging by how lucrative real estate is, this scenario will not befall you. What I am trying to say is that you cannot tap into the corporation's account for your personal needs, even if it is personal debts that you want to clear.

Loans

What you should know is that if you are applying for a mortgage as a company. That loan will be classified as a commercial loan, not a residential loan, which it will be if you are applying as a private individual. With a residential loan, you get great benefits and finance options (FHA, 3-5 % down payment, etc.) even as non-owner occupied.

If you are getting a commercial loan, it is really hard. Here are a few of the samples of the requirements for an actual real estate commercial loan. This is just one lender.

Traditional Commercial Mortgages for Commercial Real Estate

- Loan Size: No limit to dollar amount, 65% - 85% LTV (Loan to Value).
- Rates. Bank: 5% - 10% Private Hard Money: 10% - 18%.
- Terms: Up to 25 years.

- Payment Schedule: Variable, adjusting rate mortgage, Balloon mortgage.
- Fees Origination fees: 2-5%, third-party fees for items like credit reports, property appraisals, environmental reviews, etc.
- Prepayment Penalty: Not uncommon, but depends on the lender.

Qualifications for a Traditional Commercial Mortgage

- Credit Score: 700+ No recent bankruptcies, foreclosures, or tax liens.
- Time in Business: 1-5+ Years.
- Profitability: 1.25-1.5+ DSCR (Debt Service Coverage Ratio).
- Property: 51%+ Owner-Occupied.
- Down Payment: 15%+ of Purchase Price.

LTV of 65% - 85% LTV qualifies you for a loan. But it is a range because each bank has its metric for LTV. And that's because some banks want you to pay more money upfront, so you feel invested in the deal as well.

A few rules to follow are:

1. Cash is King. In everything you do as a landlord, remember that cash is king. You want to attract and keep the right type of tenants that will keep the cash flow healthy. Cash is the lifeblood of your investment, and without it, the business is bound to fail. Do everything possible to keep the funds coming. This is why you must request for upfront payments where appropriate. You must also keep your tenants happy so they will not delay your rent. You must also incentivize your tenants to pay. And when they make payments, issue invoices promptly and

correctly. At every point of your business, keep it at the back of your mind that cash is king.

2. Ensure that you get the right loan for you, be it commercial, conventional, or FHA. If you choose FHA, beware of an FHA overlay. It is the most houses the FHA backed loans would allow as a sole owner/proprietor. Don't worry about EIN# because most mortgage companies want to use your SS# for credit reporting purposes and lien positions, not EIN#.

Some tips to save you hundreds if not thousands of dollars

• Always ask for a Seller Concession in your contract: If you have it, the seller pays for part or all of closing costs.

• Always check with the town building and code inspector's office for any violations against that property. This way, you can have those code violations paid for the present owner and not you and the new owner.

• Confirm and verify everything you are told through a third party in the event you feel something is not right!

Incorporation Options Available to You

You might be very versatile in your knowledge of the real estate sector, but you will require a lawyer to handle this part of your business. However, let me show you some of the options you should expect to hear from your lawyer. I hope that these tips will help you choose the right one for you.

The incorporation option includes:

1. Corporation

There are two forms of a corporation which are S-Corporation and C-Corporation. Let's discuss them briefly.

• C-Corporation: This the most traditional of them, and big corporations commonly adopt it more. In this arrangement, the company's profits and losses go directly to the company purse.

• S-Corporation: In this type of incorporation, your business will pass its corporate incomes and losses through to shareholders. These shareholders then report them as their tax returns. But the business still remains a separate entity. Meaning that it is liable to its debts and damages. The S-Corporation was introduced much after the introduction of the C-Corporation. The federal government introduced it because they realize that small corporations and their big counterparts can face quite different challenges. Hence it was introduced to help smaller corporations because they will get the limited liability status that makes incorporation appealing while still granting them a friendlier tax environment. With the S-Corporation, you will get the tax conditions you would have gotten if you operated as a sole proprietor or a partnership.

However, to make your real estate business an S-Corporation, there are some conditions you must satisfy, and they include:

• First, it must be a US corporation.

• There is a limit to the number of shareholders it can

have. It started as 10 in 1958 and became 17 in 1976. It increased continuously with a few years' intervals until it became 100 shareholders from 2004 till now (2020).

• It might not be permitted to offer more than one class of outstanding stock.

• There are also some strict requirements in terms of the citizenship of the owner and shareholders, so find out with your lawyer if you pass the mark.

2. The Limited Liability Company (LLC)

Compared to corporations, LLCs have less strict regulations that grant you greater flexibility in defining your company. It also confers you with legal protection from liability since it is still a legal entity.

How Do You Go About the Incorporation?

Your lawyer will worry about this detail, but it wouldn't hurt to hint you on what you should expect. First, know that you may pay several hundreds of dollars for this. I would have given you a precise amount, but it varies from state to state. This fee falls into two categories, which are the initial filing fee and the yearly renewal fees.

Before setting off to incorporate, there are a few things you must agree upon because you will be asked. You need to decide on the name of your real estate business, its total number of shares of stock you will make available, and the percentage that you and the other owners can purchase. You will also provide a detail of the amount you and other owners intend to invest and the management structure that the organization will run by. Additionally, you will stipulate the bylaws that the corporation will follow.

In the selection of a business name, I need not tell you

that you must be unique, and have a clear right to it before you can use it. So, it is always best to reserve the name with the state before going off to file for a corporation. You must attach either corporation, company, incorporated or limited to whichever name you choose, to make it legal.

So remember, do your homework, ask the right questions and get the answers you need so that you are well informed and prepared to make the best decision based on the information you obtained when purchasing a house. With the knowledge you have gathered about incorporation in this chapter, talk with your lawyer or accountant, and decide on what's best for you and your real estate business.

CHAPTER FIVE: "LANDLORDING" 101
- LOOKING FOR YOUR TENANT

You have jumped into the Landlording business, and you just do not know where to start. In my case, I only bought units that had tenants already, so I didn't have to spend more money on ads, viewing, and everything else looking for new tenants while I had to pay the mortgage at the end of the month.

But in the event you buy a place with no tenant, I use only two sources that have worked for me all the time and delivered 100% of the time. The sources are Craigslist ads and ads in my local penny saver. I use craigslist first then proceed to the penny saver.

Once you get prospects, you want to pre-qualify them, I use this script to start the conversation.

Hello _____,

My name is _____; you contacted me about the unit available. (Note: Let them answer. then give them the details.)

The rent is _____ to qualify for the unit there is a rental application, and that fee is $50.00 per person over the age of 18 years old moving into the unit.

Personally, I say anyone over 18 years old because if children are living in your property, you want to make sure the criminal background check covers them.

Then stop and listen to them so that they can tell you what to find and look for on their report!

If they have bad credit, I will tell them that it may affect their Security Deposit, or they may need a cosigner. I will tell my prospects that I have two Security Deposit options, but the option they will get will be dependent on their situation.

The two options are:

1. I will take your first month's rent and one month and a half for security. Or 2. if they are borderline credit, I'll take the first month's rent, last month's rent, and one month for a security deposit.

Remember, this is a fluid conversation, so these are just my talking points, you may have your own. Just make sure you sound confident when speaking to them for the first time. Remember that the first impression matters a lot, and this is their first impression of you.

I also tell them we require the most recent pay stub for income verification. You'll get all the answers you need right here (listen to their response). The reason why you don't miss this step is that this process gives you their work information since it is confirmed on the rental application. This is critical because now you know all their financials and where they work, in the event this relationship turns "bad" or "ugly," you don't have to pay for a workplace "skip trace." You have all the information you need to garnish their wages should you go to court and get your judgment.

Once they do the walkthrough, I have my tenant application with me or the person showing my unit, so I don't have to email the application to them. If they are prepared and want the unit, they will have money right there or that day for the tenant background check. These services take about 24 hours to have the information back to you. It has been sooner in all my cases, but I say 24 hours just to be safe.

If you can get references from their previous and current employer, that too will be great. The previous employer could tell you why they parted ways, why their current employer will confirm that they are employed as they claim.

The Ideal Tenant

The sad truth is that nobody can handle your property the way you would. While some may be generally compliant, others may be defiant. You must make conscious efforts to screen your prospective tenants properly.

I know that there will be those times when tenants may be scarce, and you need to fill up vacancies just to prevent the negative cash flow, and you may have to settle for tenants that are below par. But generally, you want to end up with compliant tenants that will promptly pay their rents, obey the laws of the neighborhood, and take care of your property as they would theirs.

Apart from taking care of your property, you want somebody who will promptly meet their financial obligations. And you don't want someone who will commit heinous crimes in your property.

So here are a few things to tell that a tenant is ideal.

Stability

You can check stability by asking them how long they've been at their current job or how long they lived in their previous home. If they have been in their job for more than two years, they are stable, according to statistics. This is because their current employer will less likely let them go. After all, it is assumed that they have enough knowledge and skills that make them a valuable asset to their employer. If they are less likely to leave their current job, they will be less likely to relocate soon, leaving you with a vacancy. Also, ask them to tell you other positive attributes that they have.

Their Disposable Income

You need to be concerned about this because it tells you that the prospective tenant can pay your rent. To be safe, use the 3-times rule, which states that your tenant's gross income must be at least three times the asking rent. Since you will get access to the credit report, you can check the things they will have to pay off and ensure that the remnant is still three times the rent.

Accountability

By looking at a tenant's credit records, you can see how they treated other creditors. Did they pay in due time, or did it linger forever? You need to worry about this detail because, as a real estate investor, you are also a creditor. You need to be wary of late payments of 30 days and above. However, if this person has no late payment records, it shows they know their obligations and lives up to it. One-time late payment should not be a deal-breaker for you. Look for recent patterns that say it is a habit, if you find them, look elsewhere for a tenant.

Red Flags to Look Out For in a Tenant

They are somethings you should watch out for when considering your prospective tenants. They include:

• No Credit History

The fact that a person has no credit history means you don't even know what to expect from them. How do you know they can pay their rents in due time?

If you must accept such a person, probably because you need to, then ask them to get you a guarantor, lease, or cosigner, especially if they are young or a college student. Then to cushion for your risk, request a bigger initial deposit but don't exceed your city's limit for the maximum initial deposit.

• Tenants with High Debts

If they are deep in debt, you will find it more difficult to get out your rent when due. You may decide to bait an eyelid to it, but if you notice that the debts are escalating or occurring recently, it might get even serious in the near future.

• Tenants With Criminal Records

You can reject a tenant on this ground as it is not covered in the fair housing laws. This is not something you should joke with because if a crime occurs in your property, you will be liable for it. Besides, certain laws prohibit you from harboring a certain set of criminals in your property. For instance, sex offenders and violent criminals cannot stay close to schools or children. So if you have children in your apartment building already, you know it's a no-no.

• Tenants with a Gap in History

If you notice a gap in the residence history of your intending tenant, don't ignore it. Enquire from them what happened those years. It could be that they are trying to hide a bad situation with a previous landlord. Seek out that landlord and get a reference from them.

How to Choose the Best Tenant

Now that we know the things to look out for and the red flags to never tolerate, let me show you how you can find that ideal tenant for your property.

1. Make Your Property Presentable

Its normal logic; good properties will attract stable and compliant tenants because these kinds of people like organization. Besides, you will be using the pictures of your apartment to advertise it on sites like craigslist, Rightmove, and Zoopla.

2. Check What Other Property Owners are Doing

Are they adding new installations? What is their average price? Like it or not, this is a competition, and you have to be informed to be at the top of your game.

3. Keep Your Current Tenants Happy

Your current tenants have friends, families, religious acquaintances, coworkers, and so on. If you are treating them well, they will recommend your property to people they love whenever these people are looking for recommendations.

4. Carry Out All Maintenances

If it is not a new apartment, it is possible that the

previous occupant left some damaged parts behind while leaving, fix all of it before advertising.

5. Establish Your Ideal Tenant

When you know what you are looking for, you will easily recognize it when you see it. We've discussed the ideal tenant, use that as a guide, and come up with that ideal personality you want.

6. Run Checks

Credit Check: You want to know if they've had bankruptcy issues, evictions, and civil judgments. Also, check their income to debt ratio. These checks will cover the credit check.

Criminal Records Check: The next thing you need to look out for is criminal records. Thankfully, criminal records are available to the general public. If employers can avoid people with criminal records, then you should too. You can do this research with the following bodies:

- Federal Court Record Search
- A Statewide Criminal Record Search
- A County Criminal Court Search
- A Department of Corrections Offender Search
- Sexual Offender Database Search

Tenant's Rental History Checks: Here, you will need to talk to their previous landlords. If they did NOT give you their Landlords' information it is for a reason, they do not want you to talk to their landlord! Do NOT, Do NOT... DO NOT rent your unit if you cannot speak to the previous landlord or property manager. Make sure they are not giving you the slip and using their parents and friends as referrals, either.

When talking to the previous landlords, verify whether they paid their rents promptly, why they are moving (eviction or normal relocation). Verify how they maintained the apartment during their stay, whether or not they gave the expected 30 days' notice before leaving, whether or not they caused damages to the apartment, and how they related with neighbors and the landlord.

7. Follow Your Instincts

Your instinct is hardly wrong; if it tells you that a prospective tenant is trouble, don't sweep that feeling aside. Pay attention to it and try to find out why you are getting that notion. Even when they look good on paper, but you feel that there is something off about them, follow your gut.

How To Approve or Reject Tenants the Right Way

Now you have done all the work and found that tenant. You have subjected them to the tests and checks, and you have come to your conclusion. Whatever it is, whether to accept or to reject, there is a procedure, and that is what we will be discussing in this section of this book.

Just as it is important to accept a tenant correctly, it is also very important to reject a tenant cordially. That is because it can have legal implications, and you might not know it, but it might just be one of the most awkward things you will do in your "landlording career." So, yes, learn how to do it right.

Accepting the Applicant

Usually, a quick call, email, or text informing them that they have been accepted is okay. Use this communication to inform them of what the next step is from that point. The next step should be to have them sign a lease, so you can collect your first rent so you can communicate the move-in date assuming nothing is left to be sorted. For me, I like to text or email them that they have the unit, and then we hammer out the details for Security Deposits, walkthrough (with the apartment checklist and photos), and the move-in date.

At this point, try to get the prospective tenant a copy of your lease as soon as possible so you can seal the deal before they locate another place. This is assuming that you have done your checks, and they are the ideal tenants. Since you want to be strict with your screening and all that, also realize that you need these tenants to be in business.

To be sure that they sign the lease promptly, I will recommend that you add a deadline to it. If you don't do this, you risk losing that tenant because they may hesitate, and before you know it, they may decide otherwise. There is a reluctance that comes with moving into a new home, so give your tenant that extra push so that at every time, your property will be filled. Your deadline should span between 24 to 72 hours.

You know that if you lose a tenant at this stage, you will start the entire process again with another person, and during that time, you will be losing money by way of vacancy.

After they sign the lease, ensure that you collect your first month's rent and deposit within seven days of them signing the lease. It is this payment that invalidates the lease agreement.

With the payments made, the tenant is cleared to move in. As they move in, you can stick around to remind them of a few house rules that you expect to be always kept to avoid eviction.

Rejecting the Applicant

If, after your scrutiny, you feel that the prospective tenant is not your ideal tenant, ensure that you let them know early enough so that they can resume their search for a rental. But be sure that you gave all your prospective tenants equal fighting chance by subjecting them to the same test. That means you should request for an application, their credit reports, and then conduct a background check on them, without exceptions, prejudice, or favoritism. Fair Housing laws require that.

Fair housing law also requires that you don't reject a tenant based on the following protected class:

- Race or color
- National origin
- Religion
- Sex
- Familial status (families with children)
- Disability

Some states might have some additions to this, so talk to your lawyer to be sure that you are not breaking any law.

You may not be able to reject on tenant based on the protected class listed above, but you can on the following conditions:

- Poor credit history
- Criminal history
- Bad comments from previous landlords
- Income level

If you have checked and there are defaults in any of the points above, the next thing is to reject them, and it is best to do so in writing. This will serve as evidence showing why you rejected them if they sue you or file any complaint.

Select your words carefully. If you have found a more suitable tenant, mail or email them something in the line of, "We regret to let you know that the property at (insert address) is no longer available as we have rented it out to another applicant, thank you." Before saying you rented it out, be sure that you are not lying because they may do their findings and sue you.

If you haven't gotten someone else, but you just do not want them because they fall short of the mark, mail or text (save the text message) them something in the line of, "We are sorry, but due to the _____ on your tenant application (i.e. credit report, criminal background check, employment or landlord verification), we are unable to rent this unit to you at this time, thank you."

If you are fortunate enough to have several tenants asking for your property, split them into batches, and attend to them after one another. So that if you don't find a suitable tenant in the first batch, you can always turn your attention to the other batch. This will save you from losing all your prospects just because you rejected the second choice while chasing the first one.

Summarily, the success of your real estate business is largely dependent on the quality of your tenants. Therefore, you must pay attention to this aspect. You may do very well in every other aspect we've discussed and the ones we are yet to discuss, but if your tenant doesn't pay their rent, slam you with lawsuits, or commit crimes in your property, your progress will be slowed.

CHAPTER SIX: THE "GOOD CYCLE" - MANAGING YOUR PROPERTY

The success of your adventure into the world of real estate is highly dependent on your tenants and your financial management skills. Since that is the case, you must ensure that you keep your tenants happy always because, just as I said in the previous chapter, cash is king. So how do you keep them happy? Simple. Just ensure that their stay in your property is comfortable, then you can add the extra icing of being nice in the way you relate with them, that's all. Assuming you took your lesson on "finding the right tenant" seriously, and you do these two things, you will have wonderful tenants. They will promptly pay their rents and not cause you any trouble.

In this chapter, we will focus on how you can grant them a comfortable stay by managing and maintaining your properties in the best way possible.

There are three phases to the management of your property:

- Managing your property.
- Managing your tenants.

- Managing finances.

Managing the Property

Managing your property can save you from emergency, loss of tenants, and degradation to your property. Electrical and plumbing issues will always arise, and it will be great if you attend to them promptly before they lead to further damages to your property. When it comes to managing property, you will require the services of handymen and contractors. Let me share my thoughts on that.

Handyman

If you are just starting and you have just one property, managing your property might be easy. Still, when you start expanding as you should, it will become more difficult to look after all your properties and carry out those occasional repairs. In such a case, you will need the services of a handyman.

A "Handyman" that will make your job easier. I will also give you a general breakdown of everything you need to properly manage your properties.

The issue of a handyman is a problem with most landlords and professional property managers because, on a bigger scale, you need quality work done, and you need it done affordably. For you to get that, you must do your homework.

For me, I always start with three prospects, which I will outline below.

The first thing I do is to go on Craigslist,

While waiting on for prospects on Craigslist, I will also ask around with people I know, especially fellow landlords and homeowners, to see if there is a handyman whom they've worked with before that they can recommend to me.

The third thing I do is look through my local penny saver to see if I can find some there.

Once I have drawn a shortlist, I will interview at least three people to be my handyman. That's because I keep two of them and rotate them and work depending on what they are good at the time and their flexibility.

If you are going to be following my methods, make sure that they have all the basic skills you need, such as electrical, painting, plumbing, drywall, woodwork, etc. This will cut down on your cost of paying the master electrician or plumber to come out.

Once you have gotten your handymen, set the standards as to how you want them to work. In my approach, I usually ask my handyman to give me an estimate and take photos. If I am okay with what I see, I will tell him to proceed. As they proceed, I will require them to give me updates. Then, once they finish the work, they know they must provide me with photos of the completed work so I can keep good records.

Another detail that I like to work out with them is the modalities for payment. I'll like to know how they prefer their payment. Some will prefer paying them for work from time to time. Remember, I said that their workload is up and down. This will be an advantage to you during those times when your money is tight. It is also better for them because they get a weekly, bi-weekly, or monthly check based on the work they did, giving them income during their slow periods of work. Adopting this method has saved me from bankruptcy because my contractor would take monthly payments. You may opt for another payment scheme, just ensure that you do what you agreed on.

You cannot afford to ruin your relationship with your handyman because they can be of great value to you. If you ruin the relationship, it could hurt you down the road when you need work done but don't have all the money to get the job done. A repair that they would have done on credit, but since they are not on your side, it will cause you more stress.

Managing Tenants

You need human relationship skills to excel in this aspect. You must do everything possible to avoid those evictions that can be costly for your business in terms of lawsuits and lost rents. You need to do everything to ensure tenant retention by promptly attending to their complaints.

You must also ensure you understand and obey the prevalent landlord-tenant laws in your area. As the landlord or property manager explain anything, they don't understand in the lease and the MOST important parts of the lease agreement so that you can avoid misunderstanding, issues, or costly court cases. For instance, you know you cannot wake up one morning and ask a tenant to leave your property. You must pre-inform them of your decision.

Communicate, Communicate, and Communicate.

Now that you have your contractors or handyman in place, it is time to be proactive. By being proactive, I mean making sure the new tenant is comfortable, and they do not have any issues. There may have been things that you both missed during the walkthrough, or they may be a new issue in the unit you didn't know about. Be sure to conduct those occasional check-ins to know the condition in the unit. I need not remind you that you must relate with them amicably.

Once they tell you that there is an issue, if you have free time on your hands, go over and assess the damage, otherwise, have your handyman go over, check the place, take pictures and report back to you.

To communicate, I normally just text all my tenants, and I would get responses within a few minutes. If I don't hear

from them and it is something important, then I will call to
follow up. If you get their voicemail, just let them know you
are calling about the text message you left (give them the date
and time) and would like to speak with them. If it is not that
important, then I email them because most people have
email on their phone. If you still do not hear from them,
then it is time to stop by and knock on the door. This is
always a good thing because it keeps the tenants on their toes
and lets them know you are involved in the management of
your property.

If you have family and you can't make it, have them do it
and have them simply say, "Hi, sorry to drop by like this, but
my (in my case) brother or son (the landlord) was trying to
get in contact with you. Is everything okay? (You can even
ask the tenants living on the property next door or upstairs
do this too).

How To Spot Problematic Tenants Before They Get Out Of Hand

This is very easy to do. You drive by at different times or
have your family or handyman drive by and ask them from
time to time to let you know the condition of the property.
This way, if something is wrong like garbage in the yard,
grass not being cut, and others, you know immediately and
can address it before it becomes a problem. Also, have them
text you pictures as well, so you have proof.

When this happens to me, I normally just send a text
message saying something like, "Hi _____, I was driving by
and noticed this _____.) Include the picture in the text
message. That is what the picture is meant for so that they
can't say anything to refute what you just sent them. They
will tell you if it is theirs or the tenants next door if you have
a multi-unit property.

How To Keep A Few Set Of Ears Around If You Do Not Live At That Property

If you have a multi-unit property, ask your tenants to look out for each other and let you know anything they see or may have concerns about, loud noise, a lot of foot traffic, anything out of the ordinary. This keeps you approachable, and this keeps them honest. Ask that they send you pictures where possible if there is a concern.

How To Confirm And Verify Everything You Are Being Told

I use text messages and pictures to confirm and verify everything I am being told. I use screenshots and emails too. This gets the point across that I am paying attention to everything that happens in the property and that the welfare of the tenants matters to me.

Websites and Apps That Can Help You Manage Your Apartment in an Easier Way

We belong to a time when there are applications and websites for most of the things we do today. It is the hallmark of any serious business person to seek out valuable apps in their niche and see how they can make their jobs easier.

"Landlording" too, has a handful of sites and apps, and you will be amazed to know that they cut across almost everything you might want to do as a landlord. It cut across aspects like time-saving, renter payments, appointment scheduling, note-taking, tenant screening, accounting, and general apartment maintenance management.

Let's get right in and discover some of the best apps in the real estate niche.

- **Vacancy advertisement**

Apart from Craigslist that most people are conversant with, there are several other apps for advertising your vacancy. They include Abodo, apartments.com, move.com, realtor.com, Zillow rental manager, Cozy.co, Trulia.com, Livelovely.com, and Walkscore.

Most of these apps can help your property get that much-needed exposure. For instance, Craigslist gets a whopping 50 billion views every month. With that, you can be sure to attract a decent amount of tenants if you present your adverts properly with enticing pictures and a good unit.

They also allow you to write high-quality descriptions of your rental unit so that prospective tenants can know what you are offering. There is also a space for up to four photos that you will take.

If you are going to use Craigslist, ensure that you re-list your advert every day so that it will always remain relevant because Craigslist sorts adverts by how recent they are.

- For tracking your mileage so you can attribute costs to each of your properties, use Mile IQ.

- For conversion of currency, if you are dealing with a tenant who transacts in a different currency, use Calcbot.

- You will be dealing with several documents, and you will be sending them to different people in different units, so you will need an app for managing documents. For that, Dropbox is great.

- You will scan a lot; some will be urgent, if you have an android or iPhone, you can quickly scan, manage, and edit all your paperwork with Scanbot.

• As a landlord, you will initiate and finalize several agreements, and some will need to be done over the web. In such a case, you need an app that you can use to electronically prepare, sign, and manage agreements. DocuSign is the app for that purpose.

• With so many apps and websites for your business, coupled with social media, I bet remembering all of them will be a bit of a headache, but not with 1password. It is an app that can remember all your passwords for you.

• If you can afford an assistant, that would be great, but if you are keeping a tight budget, then Google Assistant is the app for you.

• For inspection of your properties, especially when they are many when you expand, you will need ZInspector. It helps you to document, organize, and store all your properties.

• For insurance, since risk is an inherent part of the business, Sure is the app for you.

• To know what you should charge for your property, you can use the Rentzend app.

• For your financial reports, use vts.com.

• You can locate handyman and other maintenance vendors on keepe.com.

• When you need apartment cleaners, visit hand.com.

• Experian helps you check your renters' financial prospects.

• Tenantverification.com is great for verifying your tenants.

• When it comes to online rental payments, there are several apps you can use; stripe.com and rentpayment.com are great as they enable you to give your tenants a seamless rent payment experience.

• If your handyman can do plumbing, electrical, and HVAC work, that is great. If not, a site like homeadvisor.com can help you locate professionals that can help you with your repairs.

Managing Finances

Maintaining your properties also means receiving your rents promptly and managing it accordingly. That's because you need the money to pay the property bills and effect the right maintenance, and still have enough saved up for further investments. Let's discuss the rent collection methods available to you.

1. Online rent collection

This has the advantage of being convenient for you and your tenants. However, you should ensure that you have an alternate means of payment if your primary means of payment is online.

In addition to the online rent sites and apps we have discussed, some other sites such as ERentPayment, PayPal, Venmo, RentMatic, and RentMerchant.

2. Collect Rent Mail

You can also have your tenants send their rents via mail. But be aware that some dubious tenants may try to play smart by claiming that the check got lost in the mail. To prevent that issue from ever costing you, obtain a certificate of mailing from the post office. This certificate aims to confirm that the mail was sent as the tenant claims. Or you can have a late rent fee in the lease, so the tenant knows that if they choose to mail the rent check, but it is not received by the due date, they will incur a late rent fee for that month. (Pro Tip - Make sure the late rent fee is high enough to get the attention of the tenant that they make sure the rent is not late!)

3. Drop-Off Location

You can have your tenant drop off their rents at your home, bank credit union, or if you are big enough to have an office for your real estate business, then your office will suffice.

4. In-Person Collection

You can communicate with your tenants and ask them when they have the money so you can stop by and collect it from them. This is not the best option available to you because it can be stressful establishing when both of you will have spare time.

5. Property Management Company

If you don't have the time to bother about rent collections, you can contract that out to a property management company that will do that for you. They will collect rents for you, deal with tenant complaints, and possibly manage maintenance issues if you want them to do that.

There you have them, the rental options available to you. Apart from personal preferences, there are other things you should consider when choosing an option to go with.

They include:

• The size of your real estate business: If you are managing one rental property, you can use options such as in-person collection and drop-off location. But if your units and tenants are much, then you have to settle for online, mail, or property management firms.

• How far you are from the rental properties: If you are far, use any of the remote electronic options available to you.

• Interaction with tenants: If you desire to keep close contact with your tenants, you may opt for those options that can afford you some personal time. This has its advantages as it endears your tenants to you, and you can also use those times to monitor your properties.

In summary, property management is something you must take seriously. If you are not planning to be a full-time landlord, you should opt for a property management company to do all that for you. But if you will do it yourself, which is more advisable as it saves you some money by way of unpaid commissions, then you have all you need to manage your property properly.

CHAPTER SEVEN: THE "BAD CYCLE"

Y ou may not have thought about it before now, so let me inform you that no matter what you do, you will almost certainly encounter those occasional troublesome tenants. If you are not prepared for it, it can leave you stressed out. So, the best way to prepare is to anticipate it.

So in this chapter, I will be preparing you for it before it comes. I will also show you how to respond when it eventually comes. Our aim here is to show you how to manage that bad cycle without resorting to eviction. However, no matter how hard you try, an eviction will be inevitable in some cases. In the next chapter, I will be showing you how best to proceed when such a situation arises.

Some Problems You Are Likely to Encounter

1. The most prevalent is the late payment or non-payment of rents. We will discuss that in more detail later in this chapter.

2. A building or unit has a bad reputation. If you catch wind that your property is being used for something illegal, you have to investigate it. You must resolve it by contacting law enforcement to resolve any issues with the building. If you do not act fast, it may affect your ability to attract reasonable tenants to that building ever again.

3. A tenant that is always disturbing other tenants. Remember that I told you of how people can change, and sometimes so do your tenants. If you notice you are getting more complaints about your tenants from other tenants (your eyes and ears) on the property, then you know something is wrong. This behavior is out of character for that tenant. It is time to be proactive by texting, calling, or knocking on the door of that tenant to see if anything is wrong. We encounter such neighbors every once in a while. For such scenarios, allow your tenants to resolve their issues, only mediate and see if you all can come to a peaceful resolution. If it continues, issue a query to the defaulting party, but be meek in your approach. You don't want a tenant to start thinking you are taking sides.

4. A high tenant turnover rate is also another issue you might encounter if you are not careful. High tenant turnover simply means tenants are not staying put in your property. One major reason for this is the lack of adequate and prompt maintenance. We will discuss that in more detail later in this chapter.

5. Purposeful damage. Some tenants will pay rent as when due, be peaceful with neighbors, but they will be reckless with your property. You must never tolerate that. By documenting the state of the unit before they moved in,

and after the damage, you can get them to effect repairs that were as a result of their negligent actions.

The Issue of Rents: Handling The Late Payer and Non-Payer

If you are lucky to have early birds as tenants, good for you. These people understand their obligation, and they live up to it. However, sometimes, you will encounter the late payers and non-payers.

How best do you proceed with them?

First, ensure that you included the date for rent payment in the lease you gave to them. Usually, it is on the first of every month, but you can opt for any other day within the month. Just ensure that your tenants know the due date.

The Late Payer

For the late payer, don't tolerate it. They start that way before becoming non-payers altogether. Ensure that you enforce the late payment fee that I am assuming you know you must include in your lease. If a tenant defaults just once, give them a period of grace and collect your rent. It is also a good practice to talk to the tenant, telling them what you have noticed about their late payments and asking them what their reasons might be. Tell them you need the rent at the due dates because you have financial obligations of your own, like mortgage payment, taxes, and the maintenance they enjoy.

Hopefully, you both will come to peaceful resolutions. But if they start making it a habit, you must act promptly. Even if they default by a day, let them pay the late payment fee. That will serve as a deterrent. But if you feel like an incentive is something you can afford, you can offer an incentive of 20 or 25 dollars for early birds to encourage early payments.

The Non-Payer

This category is as ugly as it gets. Sometimes, they have a legitimate reason like job loss, car breaking down and they have a big repair bill or insolvency. Other times, it's just flimsy excuses like, "I don't feel like it," or "I don't have it," even when they do. The first thing you must realize, no matter the reason, is that non-payment of rent is a serious lease violation offense, and the tenant is at your mercy.

Eviction is often very expensive and time-consuming, and we don't want it to get to that level, so we want to do everything to avoid this, and it all starts from screening. You must never play with your screening phase or conduct it haphazardly just because you are itching to fill up your rental property (Note: Every time I had to evict is because I skipped one piece of this screening process!). The other thing you can do is to ensure that you have simplified rent payment and made it as easy as it can be for them by making it possible for them to pay online, as we discussed in the previous chapter. The third and last thing is dialogue. Try asking them what their reasons are and tell them that you don't want it to get to the eviction level, and you wish that they can cooperate with you.

If all of these falls on deaf ears, I will show you how to proceed with such tenants in the next chapter.

In both cases, keep records of their payment records so that you can use it as a reason for eviction when things go south. Record their payments, the due date, the date they made the payment, and the reason they gave for their late payment.

Do NOT wait, do what you said you were going to do!

This is important when you see your landlord-tenant relationship going south. You should never wait to follow up and follow-through, but when this shift happens, you need to be proactive, prepared, and focused. If you say you are going to send a letter of a notice on a particular day, send it.

You need to be in control, and your tenant needs to see that. Stamping your authority and sticking to your guns will keep them in check because they will know that you are capable of following through to an eventual eviction should they refuse to fall in line.

I usually email them first, then post the letter on the door or put it in the mailbox. If it is a duplex, I like posting on the door because I usually take a photo and send it to myself so that I will get the internet date and time stamp as proof of delivery.

This shows your tenant you have the determination and follow-through. If this goes to court, you only have a few days to serve the notice and submit paperwork to the court before you can take action, or the process becomes null and void. You will have to do it all over again. This will amount to time wastage and loss of money, and as a business person, you don't need it.

How To Get Back On Course, If You Can; Make Nice

This is quite simple. All you have to do to get back on course is to tell the tenant that you are glad that the issue has been resolved, and you sincerely hope that it will not happen again. Tell them that now that it is over, you both should move on and restore the cordial relationship you had before. From that point onwards, be nice, but be firm also. Never loosen your grip. Your tenant doesn't need to sense weakness in you.

When addressing them for that first time, keep it short and simple. That way, you won't bring up old feelings or give an impression there are still bad "feelings" between you both.

Things You Can Do To Prevent The Ugly Cycle

In the chapter of finding tenants, we discussed the necessary background checks you can do to prevent the chance of troublesome tenants arising. I said the credit check will reveal that the rent is at most 3% of their income. I also said you need to conduct criminal records and background checks on the prospective tenants. You can refer back to that chapter if you need to refresh on that.

In addition to the things we have discussed, there are a few things you can still do to further reduce the chances of that undesirable, ugly cycle.

Here they are:

1. Assess your temperament and keep it in check

It is alright to be firm, but never be harsh or rude to other people just because they are living in your property. Remind yourself that you are in business, and as such, you mustn't do anything that can affect the cash flow because cash flow is king.

But I must also stress this point; there is no place for indiscipline in this business. Be firm and resolute. Kathy Hertzog, the president of the revered LandlordAssociation.org, had this to say concerning that:

"The biggest common mistake landlords make is being too nice. If someone says they can't pay rent today and want you to accept a late payment or partial payment, you are setting a precedent that will make it difficult if you ever have to evict them and go to court."

2. Always use a licensed specialist for repairs

You can be handy all you want, but without the right licenses, some laws prohibit you from performing works on your rentals. Hertzog also points this as one of the mistakes she has noticed some landlords doing. If you do this, and for some reason, any hazardous situation arises from it, a tenant can take advantage of that to sue you and look to win compensation, which is not good for your business.

3. Obey all the laws and building codes

While some of the laws are always there staring at you in the face because you have heard your lawyer or other home-owners saying it, some others are very subtle but still impor-tant. For instance, did you know that even if you had a no pet policy for your property, and a tenant becomes blind, they have the exclusive right to get a pet? Now, if you didn't know that and you go making trouble with such a tenant, it may cost you hundreds of dollars by way of damages.

What you should be doing is something similar to what I do, before acting upon anything, I always try to find out everything the law says about that issue. That is why I always keep my lawyer very close so that I will not transgress against the law because, if I do, I know that ignorance is not an excuse. I am expected to educate myself on everything I should. If your lawyer is not readily available and is urgent, you can always call your municipality's administration office and tell them you want to speak to the department in charge of rules and regulations for rentals.

Apart from rules and regulations, there are building codes you should adhere to, too, depending on your location.

Building codes are some set of rules that are set as standards for buildings in different locations. They are generally the same, but it is not uncommon to notice slight modifications from state to state. These laws are put in place to ensure public health and safety.

Some building codes become law when they have gone through a process and eventually become enacted. For such building codes, you will be damned to not have them in place in your property.

If anything goes wrong, a tenant might claim that it occurred because of a certain building code or requirement that is not in place in your building.

In the US, these codes are known as the International Building Code (IBC). Ask your contractor or lawyer about it and be sure that they know about it.

If you are going to be building your rental property by yourself, ensure that your contractors know and obey the building codes for whichever jurisdiction you are operating in. But if you are going to be buying an already-built property, have your safety inspectors and property inspectors assess the property and see that it is of the right standard.

4. Draft your lease

We've mentioned something about the lease when we talked about finding the right tenant, but we didn't go in-depth, so we will look at it more because it is one of those things that can save you from that dreadful, ugly cycle.

A lease is a contractual agreement between you as a landlord and your tenant, calling for your tenant to lease your property and pay rent in return. It is one of those items you will hand a new tenant before you agree to move them into your property. You must use this lease to communicate your requirements from your tenant. If they are not cool with what is stipulated in the lease, they shouldn't move in. Use the lease to stipulate the repairs you will handle and the ones you expect the tenant to take care of. For instance, you both need to agree upon who will maintain the yard and other aspects of the building so that everybody will be clear on what they have to do. Without such clear statements, actions will not be promptly taken because one party will be waiting for the other party, and time will be going.

It should also contain details on how the insurance will be taken care of. You would like to include a clause stating that the renter is to obtain renter's insurance because your landlord's insurance won't cover for your tenant's belongings.

The lease is very important because it will be pulled up in the event of a lawsuit.

You can have your lawyer draft it for you or refer to online platforms that create customized lease forms based on states. Some of such online platforms are DIYlandlordForms.com and ezLandlordForms.com

5. Record Keeping

If you've been clumsy with records and documents all your life, now is the time to turn a new leaf. The real estate business is one with a plethora of paper works, documents, and, yes, photos, and maybe videos sometimes. Whenever anything transpires, ensure you have it on record, either as written, on pictures or videos, so that you can always pull them up as evidence if there is a misunderstanding.

Take photos during move-in and move-out inspections.

By comparing them both, you can tell if the tenant has damaged anything during their stay.

Remember that it is not going to be easy for you to recall every single detail of every unit, especially when you have acquired several properties in the course of your business. So rely on records. Your memory may fail you, but records are forever. In our discussion of apps available to you, I mentioned Dropbox. Dropbox or any other cloud storage platform such as Gmail should serve this purpose. Use them to store your records in the cloud so that you can always pull them out anytime and anywhere you need them. Ensure to name them properly and classify them well, so that accessing them won't be a headache.

6. Providing a habitable space

Litigations will hardly arise if you do all you are expected to do as a landlord. There are a few safety precautions that you owe your tenants.

As a landlord, ensure that:

• You have installed smoke and monoxide detectors in your properties and that they are working fine.

• You have provided hot water and heat in your property.

• You have provided the necessary safety equipment such as fire extinguishers and floatation devices.

• You must remove old locks and replace them with new ones before your new tenant moves in to prevent break-ins.

• You must ensure that you haven't used lead-based paint anywhere in your property.

• You must rid your property of pests such as rodents, cockroaches, bedbugs, snakes, and scorpions.

• If you have any pending repairs that you can't conclude before the tenant moves in, tell them about it, and tell them when you will resolve it.

It is also your duty to ensure that you carry out routine checks around the property. Checks can be divided into three classes of monthly, seasonal, and yearly.

Monthly Checks: Check for pests and carry out extermination exercises, test the smoke and monoxide detectors and ensure that they are working properly, and check that the fire extinguisher is still okay.

Seasonal Checks: Inspect your pipes and ensure there are no water leakages; check the roofs, especially after heavy rainfall, snow, hail or wind. Clean out the gutters and trim trees that are near structure and power lines.

Yearly Checks: Check for mold by examining shower caulking and the grouts between tiles. Change the filters in your air systems. Flush out your water heater to rid it of sediments.

Away from these routine checks and maintenance, emergency maintenance will arise, and when they do, you must handle them promptly. Some common emergency maintenances are:

- Broken furnace or heater
- Water leaks
- Gas leak or the smell of gas
- Electrical issues

- Clogged sewer lines

It is also your duty to remind tenants to take proper safety measures, especially during inclement weather conditions. This is particularly important with amenities like grills, pools, and elevated porch. In the summer, they must be careful with outdoor activities that involve fire, such as barbequing. In the winter, they must take extra precautions to avoid freezing pipes.

Summarily, as landlords, our number one wish is to have a group of compliant tenants, but that is not often the case. Once in a while, we will come across tenants who will pass all the screenings we throw at them only for them to change along the line. When that happens, or should I say before that happens? Always ensure that you are keeping to your obligations and keeping your records as a landlord so that when it is time to take action, you will have enough backup. Also, ensure that you are "killing them with kindness" as you try to get them on your side because you need them in this business.

CHAPTER EIGHT: THE "UGLY CYCLE"
PART 1

HEADING TOWARD EVICTION

As landlords, we all dread eviction because of what it means for our time and resources, but sometimes it is the only line of action left. An example is when tenants have unapologetically refused to keep to their terms of the agreement signed in the lease. At such times, when every other thing we discussed in the previous chapter has failed, eviction becomes the only option. In this chapter, I will show you how to go about it.

First, you should pay attention when dealing with your non-compliant tenants. If you don't, things can go bad very fast. At every point in time, you must be in control of the situation. If you do not take control of the situation and maintain control until it is resolved, things can go bad for you. Whenever you have a situation that can't be resolved amicably or when your tenant starts talking about a lawyer, just know that the relationship is done.

If that's the case, then deal with it quickly and move on. You cannot put your business on hold because you encountered one bad tenant. Put it in your mind that that is the situation and just deal with it. Take the emotion out of it and just move forward. Realize that sometimes, tough decisions have to be made in business. When it comes to the real estate business, you have to make them even if you like the defaulting tenant.

When chasing eviction, never take matters into your hands. When dealing with a troublesome tenant, it will seem like it is easier and cheaper to get them out of your property yourself. Don't fall for this because if you do, it can hurt your business badly. It is an illegal act in every jurisdiction and in states of the country. There are rules and regulations which you must follow.

Not taking matters into your hands means you shouldn't do the following things:

- Don't forcefully remove a tenant from your property.
- Don't remove a tenant's belongings from their homes.
- Don't change the locks or attempt to lock them out of their homes.
- Don't turn off any essential utilities like water, electricity, and gas because you want to punish them or force them to leave.
- Don't harass your tenants, even if it is verbally.

Instead, handle them with care. Don't do anything they can use against you in court. Neither you nor any of your representatives should go threaten the tenant about their refusal to pay their rents. Take the emotion out of it. When this happened to me in the past, I shut down verbal communication and only communicate with them via text and email. That way, I don't say something that they can use against me. Electronic communication also helps me document the entire communication for court purposes.

If the tenant tries to disrupt your peace or that of other tenants, don't engage with them. Instead, involve law enforcement. Just call the police and report them. Apart from using this method to bring about peace, the police report can also come in handy for you during the court proceeding. It will speak a lot about the tenant's character.

Be patient and calm enough to get them out through eviction.

Things to Do When Preparing for Eviction

As you prepare for eviction, there are two questions you need to do to answer to ensure that you don't run into problems in the process.

1. Are Your Reasons Valid?

That is a key question you must answer before you set off with your eviction. I need not tell you that you cannot just evict a tenant because you don't like them. It has to be a legal reason. Either a legal reason or nothing. Otherwise, the presiding judge will rule against you, and you know what that means for your business.

Below are the legal reasons you can evict someone on:

- Failure to pay rents at all, or continuous late payment.
- Violation of the terms agreed on the lease, for instance, keeping pets when it is stated otherwise in the lease.
- Intentional damages to a rental property or damages caused by a negligent act.
- Breakage of ordinances bordering on occupancy, noise, and health.

- Causing safety or health hazards to other occupants or the property itself.

2. Do you have documented evidence?

It does not just stop at having a good enough reason; you still need to have documented proof to pursue an eviction. Otherwise, it is just going to be your word against theirs. That is why I have been emphasizing the need for proper documentation. If you are going to be evicting your tenant for late payments, have payment receipts to prove it. If you are evicting them for damages to your property, have pictures to prove it.

In addition to the evidence, ask what court documents you need to file a complaint against a tenant are. These documents vary from by state, but the common ones are:

- The lease agreement.
- Any bounced checks given to you by the tenant.
- Records of all payments showing the late payments or no payment at all.
- In the case of damages to property, provide pictures or videos.
- Records of all communication you had with them, such as emails or phone calls.
- A copy of the eviction notice that you served the tenant.
- Proof of notice receipt by the tenant. You can get that from USPS.

This is not an exhaustive list. You are expected to bring everything that can help you prove your case. If you are unsure if something can help your case, bring it along anyway. It is even advisable that you and your lawyer plan your case so they will advise you on all you need to bring to the court. This is important because when your tenants come to court, they and their lawyers will try everything to prove their innocence, but your evidence won't let that happen.

How To Make The Building Inspector Your Secret Weapon

Remember, if you are having the tenant removed because of excessive damages and they did not remedy the situation on time, then you need proof. You should have a proof for the court by requesting to have an inspection done by your handyman to document the damage.

Any photos you collected over the term of this relationship can be used to show history. Letters you wrote to the tenant about similar problems or issues work great as well. But a tip I found to be priceless is getting the building inspector involved.

I had the town building inspector involved in two cases I had where the tenants called the inspector on me to try and paint me like I was some "slumlord." In both cases, when I spoke to the inspector, I provided my proof of the situation, and I told them my history with the tenant and the present situation we are involved in. In both cases, the building inspector confirmed with email documentation that the excessive damage they saw at the unit was NOT there when they went to the unit earlier to verify the complaint!

By calling the inspector, the tenants gave me the information I needed to prove they had vandalized my property. Confronted with this email from the Town Building Inspector, the tenants could not deny the damage, and I was awarded my judgment in full!

After confirming that your reasons are valid and have the

appropriate documents to back your claims, proceed to the next step.

Present The Tenant The Formal Eviction Notice.

Before eviction hearing, it is assumed that you have given your defaulting tenant proper notice. The law that governs the period of eviction notice varies by state, but it is usually between 30 to 60 days. Look up your local laws on eviction to know the number of days that are acceptable in your location.

In most cases, it should take about 30 days to get them out of your property whether they move voluntarily, or you are having them removed for lease violations, non-payment of rent, excessive damages, or any other tangible reason. If you follow the steps the court gave you, it shouldn't be that long unless the court is backlogged, and you'll know that when you request a court date from the clerk.

The formal notice is a simple document that you can prepare for yourself, but you can have your lawyer prepare it for you, or you can download templates online. The document will contain the reason for the eviction and an ultimatum for them to fix it before a certain date or risk getting evicted.

Then ensure that you post the notice early enough to meet the requirements set by your state. The notice should be posted on their front door, and whenever possible, send it to them through a certified mail that has a return receipt, so you can be sure that they received it. Depending on your location, you may have to pay a specialized company to handle that detail for you while paying them a small fee.

Keep a copy of the eviction notice document so that you can add it to your court papers showing that you followed due process in your eviction procedure.

After submitting the eviction notice, wait for their next line of action. If you are lucky, they may affect all the necessary changes and quell your grievances. Most eviction cases never go past this stage because most tenants are scared of losing their homes. They will do everything possible to retain their homes.

Others will opt to move out before the time you stipulated in the letter. Only a small fraction of people will refuse to effect changes like paying up their owed rents or repairing the damages, and they will still want to remain in your property. It is this category of tenants that you will resume the eviction process on.

If you wait for a while and nothing seems to have changed since you dropped off your notice and they are still staying in your property, then filing your eviction with your local court becomes the only line of action left for you.

Evicting the Tenant

If the judge rules in your favor, which they should, assuming you did all I've been discussing, your defaulting tenant will be served an order to vacate the property within a stipulated time. The time will differ with local laws, but usually the range of 72 hours to 7 days. The court will provide copies of the ruling to both you and the tenant. With a court order, the obstinate tenant will have no other choice than to vacate your property.

It is always a good idea to report to court for the ruling. Sometimes, the tenant will not report at all, especially when they know they don't stand a chance. In such a case, the judge will rule in your favor without any hesitation. But, even if you think they will not turn up, still create time to be in court.

Now that they have gotten the court order, the ball is in

their court. Normally, the reasonable ones will leave before the stipulated time. But if they persist even after the deadline has elapsed, call the local sheriff's office and tell them the situation. They should provide you with a sheriff that will escort the tenant and their belongings out of your property. If you desire it to be fast, some areas permit you to pay a crew to meet the sheriff and make the removal faster. But before doing this, ensure that your local law permits it.

After the tenant and their possessions have been moved out of your property, change the locks right away to prevent them from gaining access. You will still need to change it anyway, before renting it out to another tenant. This is the end of the eviction process.

However, there may still be some lingering issues that need to be resolved, and that is the issue of past-due rent. Recall how one of your reasons for pursuing eviction might be unpaid rents. Now that you have secured eviction, does it mean that the defaulting tenant can leave your property without paying what they owe?

Well, the answer to that question is dependent on you. If you just want to let them go off like that, it is your call, but if you want to recover your past-due rents, then you can if the local court in your location allows you to file for eviction and claims at the same time. If your claim is approved, the order to pay you your claims will be included in the court order they will receive. This order inclusion is known as a judgment, and it will state the amount the tenant is to pay to you and the time limit for the repayment. Again, if the tenant is law-abiding, then you should receive your rent before the stated deadline. If they default in the judgment to pay you, you can bring that to the court's attention so they can follow it up.

But if you do not get that in your local court, a couple of other options are still available to you. One of them is the small claims court, which we will discuss in more detail in the next chapter.

The first option is to ask them politely to pay you, but I doubt that will work, even though it works in some cases. If this option fails, use the following more direct options.

Another option is to garnish their wages. By garnishing their wages, I mean going to their employer to keep giving you 17% to 25% of their wages every month until their debt is paid in full. This is allowed in almost every state in the U.S. However, some courts require that you go through them to your former tenant's employer. If that is the case, go to the courthouse and request a garnishment order that you will take to the employer.

You can also garnish their bank account. If you know where they bank, their full name, and their bank account number, then you can garnish their bank account with the backing of the court. If your tenant ever paid you through a check, then you can get that information from there.

But then you know that you can garnish their wages when you know where they work. But if you did your screening process thoroughly from the onset, you should still have a record of where they work. You can always pull up that detail and use it to recover your unpaid rents.

Summarily, eviction is not one of the easiest things you will do in your real estate career. It is a delicate process that requires a careful approach. If you get it wrong, it can lead to unnecessary delays, extra expenses, loss of case, and a resultant loss of income. You also need to avoid that negative tag of being that landlord that evicts tenants forcefully and unjustly. Avoid it because it is not good for your business. This is why you must follow the steps I have detailed for you in this chapter.

THE ABCS OF SMALL CLAIMS COURT –
WHAT YOU NEED TO WIN

In the previous chapter, I mentioned small claims courts as an alternative to the regular civil courts. I also mentioned that they are perfect for pursuing claims such as unpaid rents and damages. In this chapter, we will take a thorough look at small claims courts, and I will show you how to get the very best out of it in your real estate business.

What is a Small Claims Court?

It is a local court where you can file claims for a small amount of money (between $3,000 and $5,000), and it will be heard and decided swiftly without the normal rigors of legal representation. This court system is currently experiencing rapid growth as more and more people are needing small claims helps.

Before deciding to use the small claims court, be sure that every other thing has failed with your tenant. Be sure you have applied the three P's on them (patience, persistence, and politeness), and it still didn't work. I am repeating this because the truth is, you can save by way of legal charges and downtime. If you can avoid it, then do.

If you are using a small court or even the regular court, one thing is very important. I can't say it enough, make sure you speak with the town clerk to get all the information you need to take a tenant to court. For instance, every court has different mailing procedures, even though the state civil court requirements are the same for filing a petition. Meaning some courts will do the mailing for you while others will require that you do the mailing yourself and bring them proof that it was delivered. This is called "serving" the documents. You still could find yourself having to re-file the complaint if you miss a step. I like small claims courts because the filing procedures are not so stringent, and it is less expensive. Most small claims courts have filing fees of $15 to $25 while regular civil court fees can be $75 to $100 or more to file. Then you still have to pay a process server to serve the complaint, which can cost you another $100 to $200.

Pros and Cons of Small Claims Court

Personally, I prefer small claims courts over the regular civil courts. If you are not sure of the one you will like to use more, consider the pros and cons of small claims courts below:

Pros

• Small claims court is inexpensive. It cost less to file in a small claims court than it is for a regular civil court. In addition, you don't have to pay a fee to the process server to serve the complaint.

• It's also quick. You can get a hearing shortly after filing your small claim, and it will be decided either immediately after the hearing or, at most, within a few days. No waiting weeks, months, or years just to get a determination.

• You don't need to hire a lawyer in small claims court. (Unless your business is filed under a corporation and you have been operating the business as a corporation.) The proceedings in a small claims court are made simple so that people can easily represent themselves. In fact, that is why some states insist that one mustn't get a lawyer in small claims court, but not all states. Do your research to know what your state permits. However, don't make the mistake of thinking that you don't need to consult with a lawyer just because the rule says a small claims court does not require legal representation. Still consult with your lawyer before you make a costly mistake.

• Small claims hearings are simple and informal: It does not involve the rigorous legal procedures and technicalities that characterizes the normal court system. However, you will still be required to prove your case with contracts, invoices, witnesses, signed notarized statements, pictures of damages, etc. The burden of proof is on you.

• You can choose where to bring your small claim. For real estate purposes, you have to file the complaint where the tenant presently lives if you choose small claims court. So if they moved from the town where your property is to another town, city, or county, you have to file in that town or city where they live now. But this works for you when your tenant is taking you to small claims court.

Cons

• Jurisdictional amount limits the amount of payment for damages that you can be awarded. For instance, if someone owes you $10,000 and you sue them in small claims court where the jurisdictional amount is $3,000 or $5,000, the most you can get is $5,000 or $3,000. Since the court won't allow you to stack up complaints, it is wise to file twice, one for non-payment during your eviction proceedings and damages at a later date.

• In the regular civil court system, it is possible for somebody you sued to counter sue you. That, too, can happen in a small claims court.

• If you win your case, you can't collect your money on the spot except if the defendant agrees to pay up right there. Once you have secured your victory in a small claims court, you still need a writ of execution or transcript of judgment to start the process of getting your lost money (unless, of course, you and the defendant agree on a payment plan). The writ or judgment allows a sheriff or other government official to seize and sell the debtor's property to get your money. (Property Execution or Income Execution) (If this will happen, you will incur some costs by paying for the sheriff's services.)

Don't worry, even if your debtor isn't able to pay up right away, the writ or judgment you have obtained remains valid for up to 20 years.

You'll have to check the specific small claims rules for your state, which you can find on your state court's website. And don't be afraid to ask the court clerk about the documents you need to file to start your claim process to recover your judgment.

How to Perform a Tenant Skip Trace

Back in the days, to perform a skip trace to find someone was expensive. You had to hire a private investigator who had means and access to databases and law enforcement agencies to get leads on the subject's whereabouts, but not anymore. With the internet, you can perform the database search for a price. (You can try the free services online, but they eventually lead you to a paid site anyway.) These traces can be used if the tenant agrees with the notice to quit and leave the unit, abandon the unit once they know you were taking them to court, or you have to find them for damages. Now that they've moved out, you have to find them to serve papers to take them to court. This is where the skip trace comes in.

With these sites, you can perform a Social Security Number Verification with Past Address History for only $4.95, no monthly charges. Just create an account with a search company.

How Long Should You Wait Before Performing The Skip Trace?

Personally, I like to wait for 3 to 4 months before I do my skip traces because it takes about three months before the address shows up in any database. You have to wait for your former tenants, the one you are taking to court to put the utilities in their name at their new location.

Sample Social Security Number Verification with Past Address History search looks like this:

Subject's Search Details	
Search Date:	01/01/2004
First Name:	Mary
Last Name:	Offerman
Search Type:	Social Security
Social Security Number:	12345XXXX

First Name	Middle Name	Last Name	Address	City	State	County	Zip Code	Birth Date	Age	First Seen	Last Seen	Phone Number
Social Security Number Results												
MARY	D	OFFERMAN	10 COMMON STREET	HAVERHILL	MA	ESSEX	01830			2003-02	2008-01	9786554321
MARY	D	OFFERMAN	APT 165, 199 CAPITAL STREET	ORLANDO	FL	ORANGE	32801	1981-01	24	2001-01	2003-04	4076651234
MARY		HYNES	29 MAIN STREET	SALEM	MA	MIDDLESEX	01970	1981-01	24	1999-12	2001-11	9796559876
MARY	D	HYNES	95 PLEASANT STREET	POTSDAM	NY	ST. LAWRENCE	13699	1981-01	24	1992-10	1999-11	3155552345

What you are looking for here is the "First Seen" and "Last Seen" sections. That will tell you when your former tenants moved in and when they moved out. Once you have this information, all you have to do is drive by that property to see if they live there. Check by looking for their cars, and that is it. That is the address you serve the court papers. If you don't feel comfortable doing a drive-by, then just use the most recent address you have from the trace.

Note: Once you have this information, do your drive-by and check the address, making sure that is their current dwelling. Your only mission is to observe and report. You are NOT to get out of the car, approach the house, or make contact with your former tenants in any manner. In some states, this can be considered "trespassing" and or "stalking." If you have someone do the drive-by, make sure they understand this because it all traces back to you. You DO NOT want the police at your door, charging you on these "false charges". You lose the element of surprise since most tenants think they got away from you and left you holding the bag for hundreds or thousands of dollars in damages. Reality sets in when they get the court notice, and sometimes they will just decide to pay the damages instead of going to court. In my case, it has happened to me twice. My former tenants decided to just pay the damages instead of going to court.

Small Claims Court's Requirements

Most small claim courts require three things:

1. A **Notice to Quit**: Check your town or city requirements. Some towns require three days, while some require five days.
2. **Petition** - This is the document you file with the court to ask that they hear your case. The filing fee is usually between $15 to $20.
3. **Notice of Petition** – This is the document the court gives you (signed by the judge to the clerk) to serve to your tenant to let them know you are taking them to court.

Note: if you are requesting an eviction, then you should get a **WARRANT OF EVICTION** signed by the judge so you can send the original to the proper authority that handles eviction removals in your town or city.

How Does this Process Work? – Generally

The documents you need are:

NOTICE OF PETITION (You serve this to the tenants after it is signed).

PETITION (You sign and send back with payment to the court to request your case be heard)

AFFIDAVIT OF SERVICE (Court required proof the tenants got your notice of petition).

NON-PAYMENT JUDGMENT (This is the document the judge signs and files with the court stating either you won or lost your claim). You will get a copy also, but you need "Transcript of Judgment" or "Writ of Execution" to file this court determination with the county. This is needed to get the judgment on their credit report. Most County Municipalities only charge $20 since it is very IMPORTANT. It is IMPORTANT because this process will help other landlords after you. After all, if they do background checks, this court case will show up on the report!

Remember how we stressed on the importance of credit, background, and eviction checks. If you do that, you won't end up with a tenant who has been through this process with their previous landlords. That is why I usually tell my prospects that I'll check for credit, criminal background, and EVICTIONS!

Getting all these documents has been made a lot easier. All you have to do is go to http://www.ncsc.org and search for "Self-Representation State Links," click on the first link. "**Self-Representation State Links** | NCSC.org ."

There is a list of every state that has a (DIY) DO-IT-YOURSELF forms process. Click your state and search for the court venue you want to file. I prefer the small claims court.

Even easier, if you do not have time to read the whole pdf book file, just do a "ctrl f" search and type the word "small claims court" to get directly to the section of the book that deals with small claims court.

How To Serve By USPS (United States Postal Service) Mail And Get Tracking

By now, you already know there are two ways to serve papers to someone, which include hiring a licensed process server at a cost that varies from state to state or serving the papers yourself, which is called "self-serve." Self-serve is the only method I use because it is less expensive, and I get the results faster.

I serve all my petitions by USPS 2 Day Priority Mail

because it is under $8 to mail, and I get a tracking number. With this tracking number, you can prove the package was delivered to the person you are trying to serve papers. Once you have the delivery confirmation, print it out from the USPS website and take it to court with you.

Pro tip: I send my documents to the tenants and former tenants through USPS Certified Mail because of the return signature and the GREEN CARD I get back in the mail serves as a proof of service. If the tenant/ former tenant knows the letter is from you, they won't accept it or pick it up from the post office. That will slow you down, and possibly reset the clock on the court proceedings.

NOTE: You cannot serve papers if you are a party to the case. So, if you are filing the lawsuit, you have to have someone that is 18 years old and NOT a party in your lawsuit to serve the papers for you even by mail. So find someone you trust to follow all the directions the court requires to serve the paperwork and complete the affidavit of service.

Pro tip: I have them placed on the door and take a photo and text or email it to me, so I get the internet time and date stamp of service. DO NOT RING THE DOORBELL OR PUT IT IN THE MAIL Door. TAPE IT TO THE DOOR TAKE THE PICTURE SHOWING YOUR DOCU-MENTS AND DO NOT PUT THEM IN AN ENVE-LOPE AND LEAVE!

I just fill out all the paperwork myself, pay for the postage in advance, fill out the shipping labels USPS Flat Rate Envelopes and give the court directions to the person I want to serve the papers for me. (NOTE: some cities do this part for you if you use a small claims court. Most of the time it is included in the court filing fees)

You can find the details for your state by looking through the pdf you downloaded from http://www.ncsc.org. Even easier, if you do not have time to read the whole book, just do a "ctrl f" search and type the word "serve" or "Affidavit of Service" to get directly to the part of serving the papers you just got signed by the court.

In conclusion, remember it is paramount that you call the court clerk first in the town or city you are going to be going to court to ask about their filing procedures. This is important, no matter the court system you are using. And whenever possible, avoid the eviction rigors, difficult tenants that know their laws can cause you delays and reduce your income for the period of the dispute.

CHAPTER TEN: COLLECTIONS "GETTING YOUR MONEY BACK"

WHAT TO DO AFTER THE JUDGMENT HAS BEEN GRANTED

I n chapter eight of this book, I mentioned wage garnishment as one of the ways you can collect your past-due rents from your former tenant. It is not just unpaid rents that you may need to collect from your former tenants. Sometimes, it is payment for damages or even payment for eviction costs. It is common for tenants to assume that since they are no longer occupying your property, then they don't need to pay you anymore.

The good news is that you can collect your past rents using some established ways. In this chapter, we will look at wage garnishment in more details, and then I will show you some other methods you can use to collect your money to the last penny.

Here are some ways you can collect your money:

1. You can collect it by withholding the legally allowable money from their deposits and returning the balance if any. It is customary for tenants to give you a security deposit. From that

deposit, you can collect what the tenant owes and return the balance to them.

2. You can also sue the tenant in a small claims court. In the filing, you request the damages owed and reimbursement for the suit's cost.

3. You can also seize their other assets if you cannot get their bank information or don't have enough money. For instance, if you know that they have a car that is solely theirs and free from a loan, you can request that it be seized and turned over. You should ensure that any asset you are seizing is less than or equal to the amount owed. If it is more, you can sell it and give them what is left when you subtract the judgment amount.

Note: Irrespective of the collection method you are using, never attempt to seize assets on your own without a court backing. If you do, you can be held for theft and or trespassing. Even when you have this backing, endeavor to go through the sheriff's office.

Income Execution or Property Execution

Here's a brief overview of both executions.

Income Executions: This works in two different stages. The first stage is when execution is mailed directly to the defendant (the debtor), and they are given 20 days to make payments.

If they default on making payments or do not make any payments, the execution goes into the "second stage." The second stage is when the execution gets mailed to the employer and payments are deducted by the employer and mailed to the sheriff's office, and then they remit monthly payments to the Plaintiff (the suing landlord).

You will need to get an income execution form, you can get these online, and you may be able to get one from the court. Although some courts do not have them. Once you get a form, complete the form and have the court clerk sign the form. Then take the execution to the law enforcement department that handles this process along with the fee. You can also email it to them if that will be more convenient for you.

Property Executions: This rarely happens, but it is still an option. You can go after the bank account, but you will need to know where they bank and an account number or SSN. The bank account in some states will have to have more than $2500 in it as the first $2500 remains in the account, and the remaining can then be taken.

The next execution is where they can take the property, and there are two types of property. You can execute against a vehicle. Though the vehicle needs to be titled to them. You can also execute against real property, and again you have to show ownership of real property. Anyone you are going for must not have any loans on it. It can be somewhat difficult carrying out a property search. They can take up your time and money if you don't know what you are doing.

With both the vehicle and real property, the law enforcement department seizes the property and then auctions the property at the County House. This is just a brief overview of both executions; there are a lot more details the Sheriff Department will go over with you if you have decided to go with that method of collections.

Note: If the defendant (your defaulting tenant) does not complete the Information Subpoena completely or withhold bank information, you can ask for or file a "motion" to the court to hold them in **"contempt of court."**

"Contempt of court, often referred to simply as "contempt", is the offence of being disobedient to or disrespectful towards a court of law and its officers in the form of behavior that opposes or defies the authority, justice, and dignity of the court."

This means more pressure and trouble for them, and more likely, they will want to settle this case and pay you your money.

Wage Garnishment

Garnishment is a legal process that enables the collection of a monetary judgment from a defendant, on behalf of a plaintiff. In garnishment, the Plaintiff (the "garnishor") is permitted to take money or property of the debtor from an institution or person that has access to the property. It is slightly different from execution. In execution, money or property held directly by the debtor is seized. To do any of these two, you have to call the body that handles that in your state. If you are not sure how to find them, your court clerk should be able to give you a referral.

Some Requirements for Garnishing

Before you can garnish a tenant's wages or bank account, you must wait for ten business days to elapse according to law. This period is to allow the tenant to pay willingly. Usually, most cases do not go past this stage because the tenant will do everything within their powers to keep to the court's money judgment. That is assuming that you requested that a money judgment be added to the eviction order.

If the ten days' window elapses and you didn't receive any money, then you can garnish their wages or account. But before you do that, you must apply for a "writ of attachment on a judgment" if you want to garnish their wages. But if it is their account you want to garnish, then you must apply for a "writ of attachment on wages." For each of the writs, you are expected to pay the sum of $10 as a filing fee. Then when it is time for you to serve it, you should go through a process server, as it is illegal for you to do so. It is this server that will take the writs to the tenant's employer or bank, as the case may be.

It is also assumed that you did not just apply for a money judgment, but you also showed proof of the amount they owe you and the amount you want to be paid. What is the judgment? It is a court order that states the decision after a lawsuit.

Another restriction that applies to the garnishing of an account is that you cannot garnish more than 25% of your former tenant's total income. The percentage varies by state.

Also, in some jurisdictions, you have between five to twenty years to pursue your collection. So if you feel that this is something you don't want to do now probably because your former tenant doesn't have the assets now, or you don't have the time and resources to chase it, then you can still do that later.

I prefer the garnishment method over the execution method of collection. And that is because, with garnishment, I don't have to worry about submitting the stringent requirements of the property execution. Once you have started the process, it will continue until the entire debt is paid, or you both agree on how to continue it.

How To Use Information Subpoenas

If you don't know where your ex-tenant works and where they bank, you can schedule an oral examination, to do this, you will pay a fee of $10 and request a subpoena from the clerk. During the oral examination, you will be allowed to question the tenant under oath about their work and where they bank. You can also ask the tenant to give you documents that prove where they work or bank.

Just as before, you cannot serve subpoenas. You must allow a process server to do that on your behalf. You are allowed to include the documents you want the former tenant to bring with them when coming to court. Some courts handle this for you.

The information subpoena is a legal document that orders the debtor or other people like family, bank or credit union personnel that know them or have the information you need to answer questions about where the debtor's assets are located.

Here's the part I like: **failure to comply with this information subpoena may result in arrest and incarceration.** So, most people who know what information subpoenas mean will always comply with the court orders.

Use of a Debt Collection Agency

You can also use a debt collection agency now that you have the notice of judgment. They take 33% of your judgment, but they do all the work like asset searches to collect the judgment. So you have to weigh your options. You know it is better to recover half of the unpaid rents than not receiving anything at all. This is the last resort because it is a long process. It takes years to get your money back. Since it takes time and the probability is sometimes slim, it is best to stick with a reputable collection agency that has the experience and has worked with several landlords in your area. If you are not sure of where to find such a collection agency, enquire from other landlords. You can also ask your lawyer or accountant for a referral.

Types Of Income That Are Protected From Collection

Some accounts are not amenable to collection even when you have a money judgment. The law forbids that you garnish such types of income for some reason. The following are the categories of income:

- Social Security.
- Supplemental Security Income (SSI).
- Social Security Disability Insurance (SSDI).
- Public assistance / TANF benefits.
- Veterans' Benefits.
- Federal Civil Service Retirement benefits.
- Federal Civil Service Survivor Annuities.
- Disability benefits Railroad Retirement Act benefits.
- Annuities to Survivors of Federal Judges.
- Longshore and Harbor Workers' Compensation Act Benefits.
- Seaman's or Master's or Fisherman's wages.
- Black Lung benefits.
- Unemployment benefits Workers compensation.

In some others, such as the ones below, some limitations may apply. Be sure to speak with your lawyer or the court clerk to know if you can apply for collection to them.

- Payments under retirement, pension, and annuity plans.
- Alimony, support, or separate maintenance.
- Payments awarded by a civil court in a criminal case.

Summarily, I want you to know that there is no 100%

guarantee that you will be successful in collecting your judgment. And sometimes, even when it is successful, it might not be worth the money spent, the rigors, time wastage in chasing the collection. So, you must start by asking yourself, "how much does the tenant owe me?". When you answer that question, then check and see if it is worth the time and attention it will require. If it is worth it, then chase it with all you've got. But if it is a meager sum, maybe you should just let it go and count it as one of those hazards in any business. But then again, the decision is yours and yours alone to make.

FINAL WORDS

Most people know the positive things that real estate can do for their finances, but they are often reluctant to take that bold step. And that is because they have come to see it as a complicated business that involves countless strategizing and some lawsuits by the side. They are not wrong because, yes, the real estate world is one where you should be making the right decisions most of the time if you want to be profitable. And yes, they will be those occasional evictions, but it isn't really a big deal. Truly, it isn't as difficult as people like to believe.

I'll like to use myself as an example. I am not the smartest of guys, but I have made reasonable strides in my "landlording" career. I had to learn these skills because I didn't have the money to hire a lawyer to do my legal work for me. Right now, I only need my lawyer for consultation in some rare cases, like when an eviction is inevitable.

You should learn these things yourself, but if you just can't wrap your hands around it, and you know a lawyer that is a friend, they can help you with the legal part of your business, such as eviction for about $500 if you fill out the documents. Otherwise, it can cost as much as $2,000 in legal fees. Ask yourself if you are really prepared to be spending that much on something you can study and understand.

You have the option of just buying your properties and putting a realtor in charge, but where is the fun in that? Didn't we say that real estate is great for breaking free from the usual 9 to 5? Besides, using a realtor as your property manager is expensive. One time I enquired about it, I had quotes of one month's rent plus expenses to manage my property. Mind you, I charge $675 per month on one of my units. The Realtor was charging $675 a month to manage, plus $675 to get the unit rented and a fee of $50 to $75 to go to the property to check on it or meet someone there. So, if I had to rent that unit out through that service and let's say I had three prospects at three different times on the same day, it would cost me $675 + $75 = $750. However, if the prospect comes on two different days, it will cost $675 + $75 + $75 = $825 and 3 different days $675 + $75 + $75 + $75 = $900 and this can go on till you get that property rented.

Apart from saving cost, this knowledge is valuable, and in today's economy, you can use it to make passive income by being a property manager in your town or city and helping people in the process. Landlords can even pay you to manage their properties for them pending when you can acquire your own and start managing it for yourself.

Now, if you are going to be managing for someone, instead of charging one month's rent, you can charge 10% of the month's rent. Since I have a duplex, it would be $100 per month that you can charge. You can even charge a fee to put together the court paperwork for your clients.

I know this book is too much information in one place. I will recommend that you always refer to the chapters of this book whenever you are confused about something. Now, let's take a quick look at the key talking points of this book as a way of refreshing your memory.

We started our discussion by exploring the massive opportunities in the real estate world. In that chapter, we saw how individual investors own a whopping 22.7 million units in the country. Currently, the number of individual investor landlords is estimated to be between 10 million to 11 million. You can, and should be the latest addition. All 11 million of them cannot be wrong.

We advanced our discussion by looking at how you should proceed when you are ready to buy your first property. You should not buy a property without doing the required homework. You should thoroughly check the neighborhood and see if it has schools, social amenities, prospects of further development, and a low crime rate. These are some of the desirable attributes a neighborhood should have.

As a proposing landlord, you need to fix up your credit score to grant you easier access to funds. A good credit score helps you access more loans, and at a friendlier rate, so you should do everything you can to repair your credit score. To do this, you should start by knowing what your score is currently, then from there; you can follow the steps I outlined for repairing credit score, one of which is disputing wrong entries.

With your credit repaired and all your research into where to buy your first property done, the next key consideration is deciding whether to incorporate or not. The decision is totally yours. I can't tell you to incorporate it because I didn't at first. The key thing is doing what suits you. Some people prefer the independence and total control that comes with a sole proprietorship; others prefer the wider sources of funds and limited liability that characterizes incorporation.

Just look at the advantages and disadvantages we have discussed so you can choose the best one for you.

When you must have gone past the stage of deciding the design to adapt for your business, and you have acquired your first property, it is time to meet the most important set of people in this business – the tenants. It is time to look for them. If you are lucky to buy a property that already has tenants in them, great, otherwise, you will have to look for them yourself by putting up adverts and screening them properly. A proper screening must include a credit record check, criminal records check, and eviction check. You will do these checks because you want to be sure that they can pay their rents and not commit a heinous crime in your property that can indict you.

When the tenants are finally in, managing your property is one great tool to keep them happy and satisfied, and you must never play with it. Get yourself a handyman who will do the checks and effect the repairs that are due. Apart from property management, two other managements are very vital. They are tenant management and finance management. You must always be polite with your tenants and keep good communication going between you and them. At the same time, you should never joke with your rents because cash is king. That means you should ensure that your tenants pay up their rents.

If they are paying, fine, but sooner or later, you will encounter a problem tenant who will pay their rents late, never pay at all, damage your property or constitute a nuisance to other tenants. At such times, you need to maintain your stance and show who the boss around there is. Start by talking to them about their actions, if they turn a new leaf, great for you. But if they don't, you need a stricter option.

Eviction! Eviction!! Eviction!!! But before you head for eviction, ensure that every other method has failed. That is because eviction is not good news for your time, resources, and reputation. But if it becomes the last resort, then you must prepare very well for it so the defaulting tenant won't pull a fast one on you. Start by ensuring that your reason for eviction is concrete enough, then gather all evidence that corroborates that reason. Then serve them their eviction notice. Ensure that you work closely with your lawyer for consultation purposes.

From my experience, it is better to pursue your case in a small claims court because it is cheaper, less formal, and doesn't require you to hire a lawyer. If all goes well, your tenant should get an eviction notice to leave your property. If they have unpaid rents, adopt any of the collection methods we discussed in the last chapter of this book. You can decide to go with wage or account garnishing, or you go with execution. Whichever method you deem fit, endeavor to follow due procedure.

Congratulations, you are ready to go and excel in the world of real estate. I have delivered on my promises by taking you on an exhaustive journey through the entirety of the real estate business. If I left anything out, then it is probably too mundane to include here. I just assume you will be able to go around it on your own. In as much as you have had an exhaustive lesson, never neglect the place of a lawyer and accountant, especially if you are just trying real estate for the first time.

One of the things I want you to take away from this book is that the real estate business can be very lucrative for you if you are willing to put in the work and practice everything you have learned in this book. It is not a big deal, and I have demonstrated that with my success in the business.

If you enjoyed this information in this book and it was helpful to you please leave a review.

ABOUT THE AUTHOR

 G.E.S. Boley Jr. – He is a devoted full time father, husband and Family Man who places Jesus above all else. George is a Martial Artist, Martial Arts Instructor with Multiple Black Belts in Taekwon-Do and Hapkido. George was a TaeKwon-Do National Sparring Champion and a Member of the 2007 USA Team. He is a Defensive Tactical Training Instructor, with training in hand to hand combat, stick and knife fighting and Freestyle Grappling. He is a health and fitness instructor and trainer, certified sports nutritionist, business entrepreneur, real estate investor, property manager, business consultant and coach.

Along with training certifications George has a Bachelor's degree in Marketing and an MBA in Business. George has many life experiences and is passionate about learning and helping people in need.

If you want insider access plus this Property Management Guide, all you have to do is **click the qr code below** to claim your offer!

REFERENCES

Abdul-Samad, H. (2017, May 18). *What Is A Good Credit Score? Everything Real Estate Investors Should Know.* Retrieved from Mashvisor: https://www.mashvisor.com/blog/what-is-a-good-credit-score/

Anderson, M. (2019, May 14). *Rule #1 = Cash is King.* Retrieved from The Small Business Site: https://www.thesmallbusinesssite.co.za/2019/05/14/rule-1-cash-is-king-3/

Center, D. B. (2017, March 25). *Landlords: Judgments, Writs, and the Eviction Process.* Retrieved from LawHelp: https://www.lawhelp.org/dc/resource/landlords-judgments-writs-and-the-eviction-pr

Collins, G. (2020, June 16). *30 of the Best Landlord Apps for 2020.* Retrieved from Manage Casa: https://managecasa.com/articles/best-landlord-apps/

Court, H. (n.d.). *Landlord's Guide To Evictions*. Retrieved from Mass.gov: landlords

Dvorkin, H. (2020, June 17). *Credit Repair: How to Fix Your Credit Report*. Retrieved from Debt.com: https://www.debt.com/credit-repair/

Eberlin, E. (2018, December 30). *12 Times a Landlord Can Sue a Tenant*. Retrieved from The Balance Small Business: https://www.thebalancesmb.com/reasons-you-can-sue-your-tenant-4144242

Eberlin, E. (2019, June 25). *How to Choose the Best Tenant for Your Rental*. Retrieved from The Balance Small Business: https://www.thebalancesmb.com/the-right-tenant-for-your-rental-2124984

Elliott, C. (2018, July 17). *What Happens When You Need Small Claims Help?* Retrieved from Forbes: https://www.forbes.com/sites/christopherelliott/2018/07/17/what-happens-when-you-need-small-claims-court-help/#4823b4106f1c

Faulkner, K. (2014, July 28). *How To Handle Difficult Tenants*. Retrieved from Moneywise: https://www.moneywise.co.uk/property/buy-let/how-handle-difficult-tenants

Green. (2015, May 12). *5 Things Every Landlord Needs to Bring to an Eviction*. Retrieved from Green Residential: https://www.greenresidential.com/5-things-every-landlord-needs-to-bring-to-an-eviction/

How to Collect (Enforcement of Judgment). (2020). Retrieved from Superior Court of California:

http://www.sdcourt.ca.gov/portal/page?
_pageid=55,1555802&_dad=portal&_schema=POR-
TAL&a=3#RentalIncomeGarnishment

Johnson, J. (2020, January 20). *Collecting Unpaid Back or Delinquent Rent From Tenants: Do's and Don'ts*. Retrieved from Free Advice: https://real-estate-law.freeadvice.com/real-estate-law/landlord_tenant/collecting-unpaid-back-or-delinquent-rent-from-tenants.html

Jordan, J. (2020, 26 May). *2018 Rental Housing Finance Survey Summary Tables*. Retrieved from United States Census Bureau: https://www.census.gov/newsroom/press-releases/2020/rental-housing.html

Kenton, W. (2018, January 28). *Cash is King*. Retrieved from Investopedia: https://www.investopedia.com/terms/c/cash-is-king.asp

Lee, H. (2017, August 18). *Who Owns Rental Properties, And Is It Changing?* Retrieved from Joint Center for Housing Studies: https://www.jchs.harvard.edu/blog/who-owns-rental-properties-and-is-it-changing/

Mack, J. H. (1959). Execution Against Co-Tenants Of Real Property. *Cleveland State Law Review*, 350-358.
Marie, J. (n.d.). *How to Collect Money Owed from Past Tenants*. Retrieved from SFGate: https://homeguides.sfgate.com/collect-money-owed-past-tenants-48952.html

Meggitt, J. (2019, April 5). *Can Wages Be Garnished for Nonpayment of Rent?* Retrieved from The Nest:

https://budgeting.thenest.com/can-wages-garnished-nonpayment-rent-33544.html

O'shea, A. (2020, June 25). *How to Invest in Real Estate: 5 Ways to Get Started*. Retrieved from Nerd Wallet: https://www.nerdwallet.com/blog/investing/5-ways-to-invest-in-real-estate/

Palmer, B. (2020, April 14). *Key Reasons to Invest in Real Estate*. Retrieved from Investopedia: https://www.investopedia.com/articles/mortgages-real-estate/11/key-reasons-invest-real-estate.asp

Richardson, T. (n.d.). Landlords. Retrieved from U.S. Department of Housing and Urban Development: https://www.huduser.gov/portal/pdredge/pdr-edge-frm-asst-sec-061118.html

Savage, K. (2019, May 21). *Can You Collect Past-Due Rent Once a Tenant Vacates the Premises?* Retrieved from Pocket Sense: https://pocketsense.com/can-collect-pastdue-rent-once-tenant-vacates-premises-26472.html

Schmidt, R. (2017, November 21). How to Calculate The Debt Service Coverage Ratio (DSCR). Retrieved from PropertyMetrics: https://propertymetrics.com/blog/how-to-calculate-the-debt-service-coverage-ratio-dscr/

Turner, B. (2016, August 23). *Should You Manage Your Rental Properties Yourself?* Retrieved from Forbes: https://www.forbes.com/sites/brandonturner/2016/08/23/should-you-manage-your-rental-properties-yourself/#3153a854380d

Ward, S. (2020, January 9). *Advantages and Disadvantages of Incorporation*. Retrieved from The Balance Small Business: https://www.thebalancesmb.com/should-you-incorporate-your-small-business-2947252

Webb, C. (n.d.). *How to Get Money From a Past Tenant*. Retrieved from Chron: https://smallbusiness.chron.com/money-past-tenant-25520.html

White, S. M. (n.d.). *The Landlord Guide to Collecting Unpaid Rent*. Retrieved from Rent Prep: https://rentprep.com/collecting-rent/the-landlord-guide-to-collecting-past-due-rent/